THE Pro Keyboardist's Handbook

TIPS AND TOOLS
TO SURVIVE AS A WORKING KEYBOARDIST

JON DRYDEN

Alfred, the leader in educational publishing, and the National Keyboard Workshop, one of America's leading contemporary music schools, have joined forces to bring you the best, most progressive educational tools possible. We hope you will enjoy this book and encourage you to look for other fine products from Alfred and the National Keyboard Workshop.

This book was acquired, edited and produced by Workshop Arts, Inc., the publishing arm of the National Guitar Workshop.
Nathaniel Gunod, editor
Michael Rodman, editor
Gary Tomassetti, music typesetter and assistant editor
Timothy Phelps, interior design
CD recorded at Bar None Studios, Northford, CT

ISBN 0-7390-1126-X (Book)
ISBN 0-7390-1128-6 (Book & CD)
ISBN 0-7390-1127-8 (CD)

Table of Contents

About the Author

Jon Dryden was born in Santa Cruz, California, where he began piano lessons at age five. While in high school, he studied with jazz piano great Dr. Billy Taylor and performed at jazz festivals in Europe and Japan. At the Monterey Jazz Festival, he performed with the California High School All-Star Jazz Band, enabling him to play alongside greats like Clark Terry, Red Holloway and Bill Berry. He graduated with a B.A. in Piano Performance from the Berklee College of Music, where he studied arranging and composition with Herb Pomeroy and John Bavicchi; while there, he also played with Pat Metheny, Gary Burton, Phil Collins, Joe Zawinul and many others. In 1991 he moved to Brooklyn and began playing in the New York scene. He has recorded or played with Michal Urbaniak and Urbanator, Paula Cole, Lenny White (featuring Michael Brecker and Victor Bailey), Regina Carter, David Byrne, Arto Lindsay and others. He is in demand as a sideman and studio musician, and performs regularly in New York with various groups and in the bands High Noon and Cocktail Angst.

Introduction

Welcome to *The Pro Keyboardist's Handbook*. This book is designed to help keyboardists of all levels understand what is involved in having a career in music. It covers musical topics and aspects of life in the musical world that aren't usually found in other books. Being a creative and business-savvy musician requires intuition gained through years of experience. This book can help you learn what you need to work on as a musician and as a businessperson. However, there is no substitute for real-life experience, so this book should be used as a launching pad for your excursions into the wide and varied world of music.

To get the most out of this book, it is recommended that you have a good working knowledge of all major and minor scales and key signatures. You should be able to read music and to sight-read at an intermediate level. If you need to study these topics, check out *The Complete Jazz Keyboard Method*, *The Complete Blues Keyboard Method* or *The Complete Rock Keyboard Method*, all published by Alfred and the National Keyboard Workshop.

There are things discussed in this book that most veteran musicians learn from experience. You can learn about these concepts, but don't assume you know everything just because you've read this book. Furthermore, not every topic addressed here will be meaningful to you, depending on what you do with music. However, it's good to read every section in order to be familiar with a topic in case it suddenly comes up in the real world someday.

The emphasis here is on helping you through real-world situations; all the music theory and business theory books in the world won't help you deal with real life. To the degree that you can, get out there and play with other people and try to put yourself in professional situations. Music is not an easy profession (or even an easy hobby), so the more you explore its powers with other people and in actual professional situations, the more you will grow as a musician.

The book is organized in chapters, each discussing an aspect of music, the music business or just practical things that every working keyboardist should know. Some of the information in the chapters on the music business is subject to change. As of this writing, there is a fair amount of turmoil in the record industry, and technology is shaping our lives in ways that are getting harder to predict.

Music is a difficult business, and there have been many casualties from bad business decisions or the acts of unscrupulous businesspeople. Don't be put off by the number of hard-luck stories you hear. If you want to succeed in music, keep your eyes and ears open and, of course, practice, practice, practice. As Oscar Wilde wrote: "All of us are lying in the gutter, but some of us are looking at the stars."

Best of luck!

DEDICATION:
To Smith Dobson, a brilliant jazz pianist, for all that he taught me and countless others.

00

Track 01

A compact disc is available with each book in this series. Using these discs will help make learning more enjoyable and the information more meaningful. The CD will help you play the correct notes and rhythms and aid with the feel of each example. The track numbers below the symbols correspond directly to the example you want to hear. Track 1 will help you tune to this CD.

Chapter 1

CHOOSING YOUR EQUIPMENT

A major aspect of being a modern-day keyboardist is—surprise!—owning keyboards. There is a constant struggle to keep your equipment up-to-date and your sounds current. Technology is constantly changing, and many keyboardists want to have all of the latest gear. While major revolutions in synthesizer technology are not happening now as quickly as they did in years past, there will always be some new product that seems better than what you already have.

Keyboard players have it rough. Other musicians expect us to know everything and to always have the proper sound for a particular musical moment. Guitarists have six strings, but keyboardists have as many as 88 keys. All of those buttons to push and sounds to know—what is a keyboard player to do?

The first thing to do is to figure out exactly what gear you need in order to perform your music the way you want. If money is a factor, you will also need to figure out the cheapest way to do it all without sacrificing too much.

KEYBOARDS

Different musical styles call for different keyboard setups. A jazz piano player will probably not need a $5000 synthesizer, and a Top-40 keyboardist will probably be unhappy with just a digital piano. Here are several different types of keyboard to consider:

PIANOS

The piano has been around for over 200 years but hasn't really become any more portable in that time. However, recent developments in the digital piano realm have made it cheaper and easier to have an instrument that both sounds and feels good. A digital piano usually consists of 73 to 88 weighted keys with a variety of sampled piano sounds from which to choose. These pianos can weigh anywhere from 40 pounds on up, and cost anywhere from $800 to over $3,000. Some have features you may not need, so a careful look into what each model offers is recommended—especially if you're shopping on a limited budget. In general, look for an instrument with a good piano sound and feel, MIDI ports (both in and out) and a weight you could tote a few blocks if you really had to (e.g., if your car breaks down or you must rely on public transportation).

ELECTRIC PIANOS

Although samplers and digital pianos have largely displaced them, there are still many keyboardists lugging around dinosaur keyboards from the 1970s. The two most popular electric pianos from that era are the Fender Rhodes and the Wurlitzer. Each has an instantly recognizable sound that many keyboardists find impossible to duplicate with a sampler. Depending on your needs, one of these models might be good for your live rig, but only if you find that it defines your sound. Less picky players will find most synthesized or sampled electric pianos sufficient. They're also a lot easier to carry around than a Rhodes.

SYNTHESIZERS

The term "synthesizer" (often shortened to "synth") applies to any keyboard that creates its sounds electronically through the use of oscillators, filters and all sorts of other things most of us never fully understand. Suffice it to say that synths can create a wide variety of sounds, both electronic and acoustic in character. There are many different types of synths, with a main distinction being *digital* or *analog*. The synths of the 1970s and early 1980s were primarily analog. When Yamaha introduced the DX-7 in 1983, it was the first affordable digital synth. Today, most synths are digital in some respect, but the warmer sound of an analog synth can be emulated with digital technology. Some synths, known as *workstations,* are all-in-one machines. They combine multitimbral capabilities (meaning that more than one type of sound can be played at a time) with an on-board *sequencer,* a device that enables you to create entire songs with drums and other instruments through just one unit. This is great if you want to do some sequencing for a live gig, or if you just can't afford a computer-based sequencer.

ORGANS

The granddaddy of all electric organs is the Hammond B-3, usually amplified by a Leslie rotating speaker. The sound of this combination is legendary, but moving either piece of equipment is only slightly easier than moving a house down the street. Most synths have decent organ sounds that will satisfy all but the die-hard organist. There are also a number of portable organs on the market that emulate the B-3 with its drawbars and settings. Other organs that have achieved a certain notoriety are the Vox and the Farfisa. Both of these have a different sound than the B-3; both sound cheesy to some people, amazing to others. They were most popular in the 1960s as cheaper and lighter alternatives to the B-3.

OTHER KEYBOARDS

There are many other kinds of keyboards out there that you can use in interesting and creative ways: the Clavinet, the mellotron and its cousin the Chamberlain, the melodica and, of course, Uncle Murray's favorite, the accordion, which is enjoying a renaissance. One easy way to get to know the sounds of all of these instruments is to find patches on synths that recreate them.

SAMPLERS

A sampler is really just a digital tape recorder. It copies the sound of something played into it and stores it so it can be played via a keyboard. Samples can be used in many ways, either each individually as a copy of an existing instrument's sound (like the aforementioned Fender Rhodes sample) or together, with several different sounds combined into one. For instance, you could combine a sampled string sound with a more synth-like patch to create an interesting layer for a song.

MODULES

A sound module is really just a synth or sampler with no keyboard. A module is considerably smaller and cheaper than a synth with keys. A MIDI cable connects a module to a master keyboard, which then controls the sound coming from the module. A drawback to having a module is that a lot of the buttons and controls are hidden within other buttons and controls to save space. Some people don't like using them in a live rig, as you can't always see or control the knobs while playing the master keyboard. But for building up a MIDI studio, modules are indispensable; more about them later.

AMPLIFICATION

There are many ways to amplify your keyboards. Keyboard amps have become popular and more compact, and they are good at capturing much of a keyboard's dynamic range. You can also get a small PA system to create a little more clarity in your sound. A keyboard amp is a good first amp, but make sure you like the sound before you buy one. Also, pick it up to feel its weight—remember that you'll have to carry it! Check the power rating to make sure it can put out enough juice for your situation. Keyboard amps require more power than guitar amps, so a 60-watt keyboard amp won't sound as loud as a 60-watt guitar amp. The differences between the two types of amps are that the keyboard model will provide a cleaner sound and can handle lower and higher frequencies better than the guitar amp.

STANDS AND SETUPS

After a while, using an old card table as a keyboard stand just isn't a good idea. There are many types of stands made especially for keyboards, and they come in different styles and, of course, prices. If you plan on having one keyboard, a single-tiered stand should be fine. Some keyboardists prefer to play standing up, while some prefer the traditional sitting-down approach. Use whichever method works for you.

If you have a two-tiered stand or more than two keyboards, make sure that each keyboard is at a comfortable playing level. A keyboard placed too high or too low will make it difficult to play and may cause tension in the arms, neck and shoulders. You should be able to see all of the readouts of your keyboards without craning your neck or straining your eyes. If you have more than two keyboards, make the keyboards on the lower level even in height—this will make it easier to switch from one to another.

When you set up, you'll want your amplifier or speaker to be as close to you as possible without it being right on top of you. Place it either behind you or slightly off to the side. This will make it easier for you to hear and allow you easy access to controls and knobs during a gig. It's often a good idea to elevate the amplifier somewhat so that it is closer to your ears and so that the sound projects to you and the crowd rather than straight into your legs or back.

Here is a typical and generally effective layout for your gig setup:

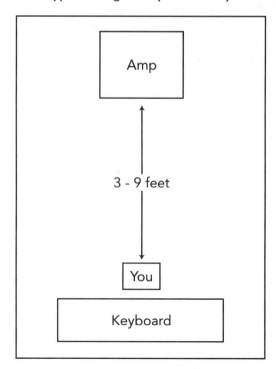

If you're getting a rig together for the first time, you'll probably want to base your setup around one keyboard, most likely a synthesizer of some sort. Chances are you probably already have at least one keyboard. If not, here are some ideas for what to look for in an instrument.

1. **A wide variety of good sounds.** A modern-day synth should be able to emulate a number of acoustic instruments, such as pianos, strings, organs, drums, etc. Some synths focus on creating purely synthesized sounds, which is great if that is what you need. But if you want something that can emulate other instruments or even other synthesizers (e.g., Moogs, Oberheims, etc.), then you will probably need a keyboard that replicates these sounds fairly well.

2. **An action that feels right to you.** If you have grown up playing piano your whole life, a light keyboard action might not appeal to you. Take some time to play a particular keyboard at a music store before you buy it. Hearing a demo or reading a great review will not allow you to judge whether or not a particular keyboard is right for you.

3. **Multitimbral capability.** Multitimbral synths can play more than one kind of sound at once if you use the "multi" mode with a sequencer. If you plan on using a synth only as a live keyboard, this feature is generally not a necessity; for studio work, however, it is a must.

4. **Touch sensitivity.** Most keyboards now have touch sensitivity, which means that the harder you strike a key, the louder the sound that is produced. Not all sounds in a keyboard have this programmed into them, and not all need it. Classic analog synth sounds have a history of lacking touch sensitivity (touch sensitivity wasn't widely available until the early 1980s), so newer synth sounds modeled after the classic synths will often have the touch sensitivity disabled. Touch sensitivity is most useful in patches like piano or electric piano sounds, or acoustic simulations in which different degrees of dynamics and attacks are needed.

5. **A fit with your budget.** The first synth you buy doesn't need to be the be-all-and-end-all keyboard of your rig. Besides, keyboard technology changes so quickly that today's hot synth will sound mediocre in a few years. Find one keyboard that fits most, if not all, of your needs, and get to know it inside and out. Read the manual carefully and *really learn* how to work with the existing sounds and create new ones. Many keyboardists and producers started out with a small amount of gear and have gotten to know their equipment so well that their music sounds like it came from a rig five times the size and price. Shop around—compare different prices and keyboards. Don't believe every salesperson you speak to; for one reason or another, he or she may be pressuring you to buy something you don't need.

Chapter 2

USING YOUR KEYBOARD'S SOUNDS

You might have noticed in your keyboard manual that you are told what a sound is like, but not how you could or should use it. That's because creativity cannot necessarily be taught. Perhaps the manual wasn't written by a creative musician. So, how do you use the sounds you have at your disposal in your synthesizer?

Most modern synthesizers have a broad spectrum of sounds to choose from. Many keyboards come with hundreds of built-in sounds, plus room to create and program your own. It can all be overwhelming, but don't despair quite yet. Let's first look at a few basic varieties of sounds.

KEYBOARD INSTRUMENT SOUNDS

ACOUSTIC PIANO SOUNDS

Keyboard sounds, not surprisingly, emulate different types of keyboard instruments. Generally, the most important sound is that of the granddaddy of all keyboards, the piano. Keyboard-produced piano sounds, whether sampled or synthesized, will most likely allow for touch sensitivity, a full dynamic range and a clear sound. Hopefully, they will also sound like pianos. Piano sounds can be straight or contain a "pad" (an additional layer). Straight piano sounds will be designated by descriptions like "bright," "warm" or "medium" layered sounds will have names like "Piano Pad," "Piano/Strings," "Piano Layer" and so on. The timbral differences among these can be drastic. For live gigs and louder musical environments, a bright piano setting (one with an abundance of high frequencies) can work well. Layered timbres work best in situations requiring a smooth harmonic sound coupled with a strong, moving melodic voice. These sounds are ideal for pop ballads and other songs in which the keyboard plays an important role.

You can do many things with a piano sound; it is probably the most versatile keyboard sound you have. The percussive attack allows the sound to cut through even the heaviest of accompaniments, while the mellow ring from the piano strings provides that sustained sound that is so familiar. When a sound like this contains a wide range of dynamics and attacks, the different colors you can achieve are seemingly innumerable.

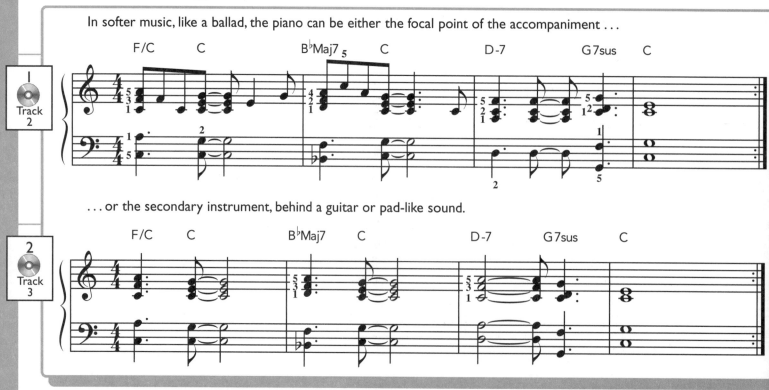

In softer music, like a ballad, the piano can be either the focal point of the accompaniment . . .

. . . or the secondary instrument, behind a guitar or pad-like sound.

Example 1 shows the piano's ability to establish the harmony while providing a rhythmic foundation. Example 2 lays out the chords with no movement between them. You could think of these examples as repetitions of the same section. Example 2 could be used in Verse 1 of a song, and Example 1 could be used in Verse 2. The simple chording of Example 2 would probably work best in an early section of a song, as it is simpler and allows for a piece to build. The rhythmic nature of Example 1 might be better suited to a later section of a song, (i.e., after it has built itself up dynamically). By subtly varying your piano arrangement from section to section, you can create a piece of music that is not only more interesting, but also builds as it goes along and contains more dynamic contrasts and a more interesting contour.

For mid-tempo songs, you can use the piano in many different ways, whether to lay out the chords in a simple fashion (Example 3A), add some small accents (Example 3B) or play a static eighth-note figure (Example 3C).

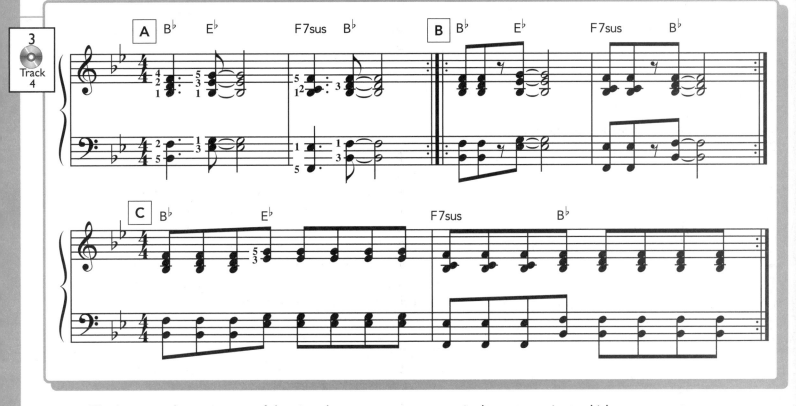

The beauty and transparency of the piano becomes most apparent in the upper register, which starts roughly two octaves above middle C. The bell-like tones of these notes can be very effective in certain passages, such the rolling arpeggio in Example 4A and the static rhythms of Examples 4B and 4C.

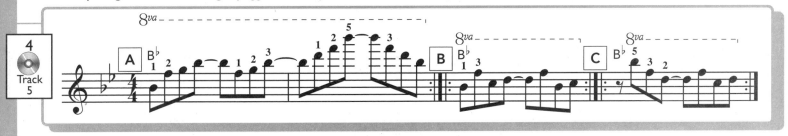

These ideas will not overpower other instruments, but will instead stand out in an arrangement. Use them with discretion, however. Overkill can be a factor when a certain range is used too often.

You can also double a bass line, either in part or in full, to thicken up a sound. Another idea is to play the root of a chord strongly. This works best at the beginning of a section or phrase, and works even better when the harmony preceding it is slightly different and the harmony following it doesn't change for several bars. In other words, it's best to let the notes ring for maximum effect:

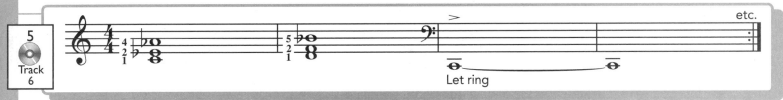

ELECTRIC PIANO SOUNDS

Electric piano sounds are labeled with names like "E. Piano," "Rhodes," "Wurlitzer" and so forth. A more trebly sound will have the word "tine" in it (tines are the tone bars used in most electric pianos). A tine-like sound is crisper, as opposed to the warmer sound of, say, 1970s electric pianos. The term "FM Piano" refers to an even brighter electric piano sound; the Yamaha DX-7, which uses digital FM (frequency modulation), spawned a slew of electric piano sounds in the 1980s. These sounds are easily recognizable and work well as an addition to a pad or string sound.

In a situation that requires a strong sound, a percussive attack works best. Try these examples using a sound with a percussive attack.

The two electric piano sounds that are most often reproduced are the Rhodes and the Wurlitzer. The Rhodes sound is generally recognizably thick. The Wurlitzer has a strong attack and a thinner sound, enabling it to blend into a track more easily.

A percussive attack can still be used in electric piano sounds in a less "active" section of a song, as long as the sound has some sustaining power. The attack cuts through the instrument mix, while the sustaining power of the sound carries the harmony. These patterns are good for these purposes and can be used in many different situations.

−= Tenuto
(sustained)

> = Accent

A warm electric piano sound works well for pop and R&B ballads. It can be the focal point of the arrangement . . .

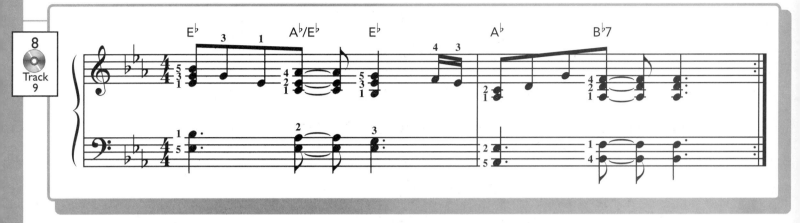

. . . or fulfill a supporting role alongside a guitar or other sustaining sound.

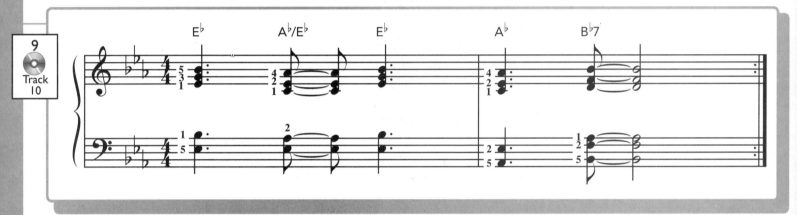

Notice how the first example above is busier and more rhythmic. As you play the second example, imagine a string pad or similar sound behind your part.

ORGAN SOUNDS

Organ sounds vary widely, from Hammond B-3 emulations to the church pipe organ sound we all know and fear. Some Hammond emulations will be smooth and clean, ideal for slower or mellower music, and some will have built-in distortion that begs you to play it as loudly and obnoxiously as possible.

Organ sounds tend to have similar shapes—that is, they always have an immediate attack when you depress a key and an immediate release when you let go of it. They also sustain indefinitely as long as you keep a key depressed. Otherwise, the sonic possibilities of organ sounds are endless.

You can use a mellower organ sound for slower ballads. These sounds should not be too heavy, distorted or overpowering. Using the basic elements of voice leading, you should be able to create a part that seems like it never moves, even though it does.

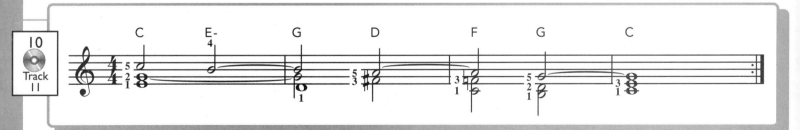

A slightly more percussive sound can be used in a more rhythmic setting. Play these examples with a percussive organ patch, accenting the staccato nature of each phrase.

The most powerful organ is one with a downright nasty and distorted sound. If you have a screamingly loud and ugly organ sound in your keyboard, try this: play a glissando up to the highest note and hold it. If it's a well-programmed and/or well-sampled sound, you will feel the power of the real B-3. The real thing seems to weigh as much as a cow, so the advantage of a good substitute is clear.

Play this example, holding the high B with your fifth finger while playing the lower notes with your left hand.

For a more rhythmic and upfront approach, try the following variation.

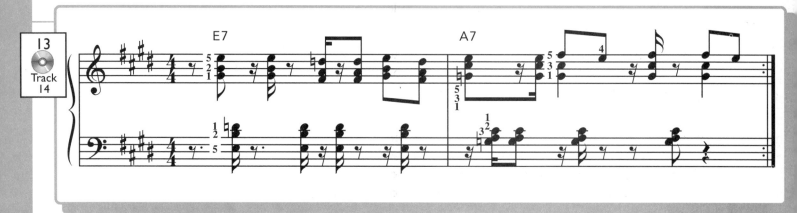

The sonic possibilities of the organ are seemingly inexhaustible. Organ sounds can range from a screaming monster to a mild pad. They're also wonderful when layered with modern pad sounds, effectively combining the attack and sustain of the organ with the warmth and sustain of a pad.

HARPSICHORDS, CLAVINETS ("CLAVS") AND MELLOTRONS

Harpsichords, Clavinets and mellotrons are all real keyboard instruments that synthesizers emulate. A harpsichord has strings much like a piano; unlike a piano, though, the strings are plucked by quills instead of struck by hammers, resulting in a more staccato sound. A Clavinet is basically an amplified harpsichord. The mellotron is a keyboard from the 1970s that uses analog tape loops containing samples of different acoustic instruments. It has a recognizable sound often emulated in synthesizers.

OTHER INSTRUMENT SOUNDS

Synthesizers also emulate a wide variety of other instruments, with mixed results. It's difficult to capture and/or replicate all of the subtleties of all acoustic instruments. Some wind instruments, like trumpets and saxophones, are hard to duplicate with synths and samplers. Other instruments, such as strings, percussion and some woodwinds, can be imitated fairly well. If you want to use a sound modeled on an actual instrument, it's helpful to learn about the instrument—its range, the way in which it is played, and so on. This will make your use of the sound less artificial, and this information is useful to know even if you don't necessarily want the patch to sound like the instrument. Drum sounds, in particular, sound better if they are played with some idea of how real drums are played.

USING PADS

Pads are smooth, string-like sounds that can fill out the harmony of a song. They work especially well in slower tempos or in sections where other instruments are more percussive; they can smooth out the sound of the song as a whole. Some pads have a "violin-ish" sound to them, while others sound more electronic or synthesized. Labels such as "Strings" and "String Pad" denote a more acoustic string pad sound. Other pad sounds can vary widely in sound and timbre. Some will have a slow attack, meaning that the sound is not heard immediately after striking a key. These slower-moving sounds work best in songs or sections with slower tempos or those that don't require sharp attacks. Other sounds will have a long decay or release, meaning that the notes will linger after you let go of them. Each pad sound has its own characteristics which can be understood only by listening to it and judging whether it works well in a particular musical situation.

Play through each of your synth's sounds. Keep an ear out for pad sounds that you like and think will be useful. Write down the name and location, as well as a brief description (big, warm, transparent, etc.) of each. When you have this information in front of you, you'll be able to move from sound to sound quickly, which is helpful when you either are unfamiliar with a piece of music or wish to use many different sounds within a song. For example, you may wish to use a thinner sound for the first verse of a song and then bigger or broader sounds for the following sections as the song builds in intensity and dynamic level.

In addition to changing sounds, you can also vary your voicings, making them denser for louder sections and sparser for softer sections. This is a more "organic" way to control dynamic levels without having to resort to the volume controls.

Use the chord progression at the top of page 16 to practice changing your pad sounds. Use a softer and more transparent sound for the first two verses, and then change to thicker and heavier sounds as the song progresses and grows in dynamic level and intensity. Try not to use sounds that are *too* different from each other, as you should ideally create smooth transitions between sections. Use a bigger sound for the second chorus than you do for the first.

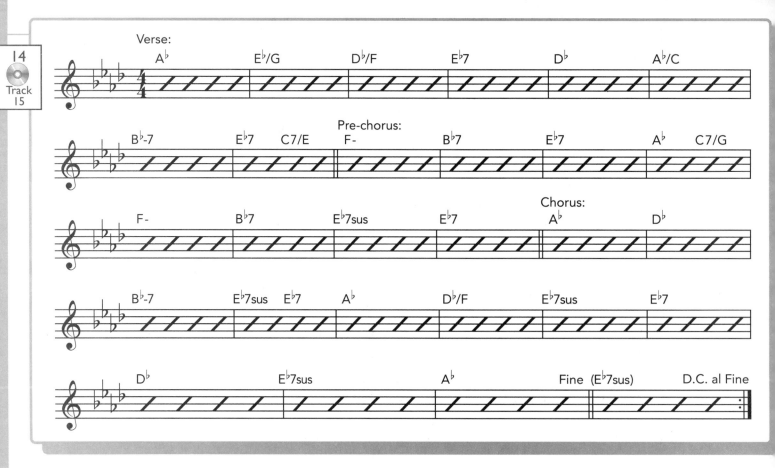

Here are some ideas to use to create natural dynamics with your voicings. For softer sections of a song, a voicing of only two notes will work quite well. Add notes as the song progresses, and vary the spacing between the notes.

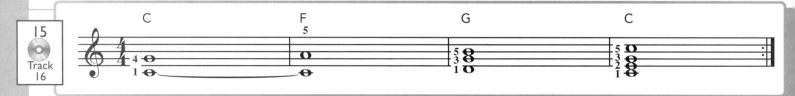

Try spreading your voicings over more than an octave using simple voice leading. This will give the impression of space while still defining the tonality.

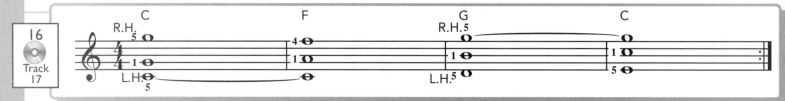

A simple triad will work well for louder sections of a tune, especially if you add the root and 5th to the bottom of the voicing.

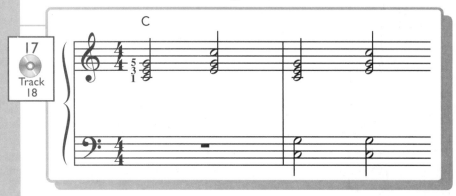

Practice combining these elements in various ways using the chord progression at top.

SYNTHESIZED SOUNDS

You've already used some synthesizer sounds in your pads, but there are many different synthed sounds that modern synthesizers can produce. This is really where the instrument gets a chance to shine. Some sounds are warm, others crisp, but they all have an electronic feel. The range of textures is tremendous, from mild pad-like colors to unearthly sonic shapes. Special effects and noises also fall into the category of synthed sounds; they have seemingly unlimited sonic possibilities. Some sounds are labeled with names like "Synth Piano," "Synth Organ" or "Synth Pad." These names can mean that the sounds on which they are based are further modified by other electronic sounds. Again, exploring the different sounds and what they can do is the only way to really learn about them and determine how and where to use them.

Synthesizers have come a long way since the first Moog synths appeared in the 1960s. It took time for them to gain acceptance by musicians and listeners, but by the mid-1970s, synths could be found in many recordings. Now they are everywhere, in everything from mellow new-age music to hard-hitting techno. They play drum sounds and orchestra sounds, as well as many "invented" sounds you may have never heard before.

DIFFERENT TYPES OF SYNTHESIZED SOUNDS

There are too many types of synth sounds to cover all of them within the scope of this book, but here are a few basic categories as well as ways in which they can be used.

Analog-style synth sounds cover a wide sonic spectrum, but they have some common elements. These patches have a warmer (as opposed to a more metallic) sound, an immediate attack and a slight brassiness. They are best for powerful chording and some lead lines. Try these ideas with several different analog-style sounds.

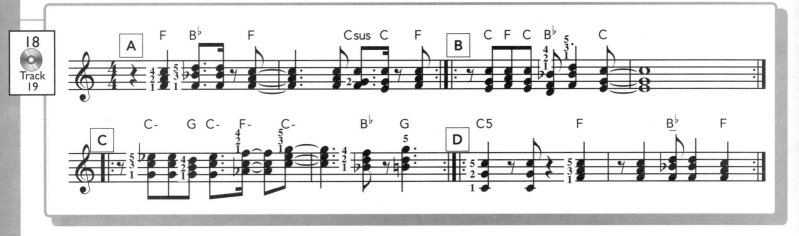

Some patches are more percussive, somewhat like the sounds produced by a guitar or Clavinet. These are ideal for syncopated comping rhythms, especially when they are played staccato.

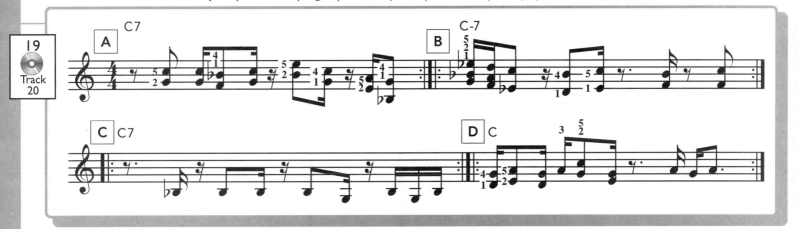

Special effects can be imitations of real sounds—like helicopters or nuclear explosions—or can be manufactured wholly from someone's imagination. Every synth has a few of these sounds; they can be fun to play with at first, but they have limited usefulness. If you do use a special-effect sound, it's best to do so sparingly.

A *sweep* sound is a cross between a pad and a special effect. The fundamental (root) tone will be present, but there will also be a filter sweep that attacks as the keys are held down. Some sweep sounds can make your synth sound like it is being sucked down the funnel of a tornado. Sweep sounds based on the root or a two- or three-note voicing work well at beginnings of phrases. Still, as with all special effects, they should be used with discretion.

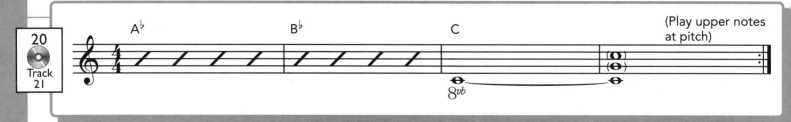

A *lead* sound is a patch designed for solos or other melodic parts. Lead sounds are generally monophonic (i.e., only one note can be played at a time) and have an immediate attack. Some are big in sound, some subtle. When you use a lead sound, make sure that it works well with the mood of the song. A loud, cutting patch might not mesh well with a smooth ballad, and a dreamy lead sound probably won't cut through a louder, driving song.

Lead sounds are most effective when you use your keyboard's pitch-bending and modulating capabilities. Set your pitch-bend range to one whole step—this will make the pitch bend a whole step in either direction. You can think of the pitch bender as producing an effect similar to that of a guitarist bending a string (guitarists often bend their strings up a half or whole step to make the sound more expressive). Try this exercise, bending up on notes as indicated.

When mastered, this technique can offer new levels of expression. In addition to pitch bending, you can also introduce *modulation* into the sound. When you add modulation through the use of either a mod wheel or a joystick, the distance between sound waves changes. The more modulation you add, the heavier the vibrato effect. Try this exercise using modulation at the points marked with an "X."

Listen to other synth players for soloing ideas, especially in the way of pitch-bending and modulation techniques. These techniques give you powers of expression much like you would have with an acoustic instrument, and can be very effective in making your solos sound more natural.

Chapter 3

Setting up a studio of your own is a relatively easy and (mostly) affordable task. MIDI has made sequencing multiple keyboards and modules a practical way of creating your own music with top-quality sound. Creating music at home is now cheaper and easier than ever before. The setup requires a certain financial investment, but it can be well worth the price if you want to record your own music or hire yourself out to record and/or produce the music of others.

Wondrous new gadgets that make you green with gear envy seem to come out on a daily basis. However, if your budget is somewhat constrained (as most budgets are), you'll do well by sticking to the basic elements of a MIDI setup.

BASIC GEAR

There are a number of items of equipment necessary for a MIDI rig of any size. Most gear is available in a variety of brands and prices. A higher price usually indicates higher quality, but there are inexpensive models of just about everything that will work well for both beginning and advanced applications. Do your research before you buy a piece of gear—read reviews in magazines or on-line, or ask MIDI-savvy friends to recommend gear. You can also save money by buying used gear, but make certain it's working properly before you buy it.

Here are the elements of a basic MIDI setup:

1. **Something to record to**. This is essentially a means of storage for your music—a way to save it for playback. You can go the cassette four-track route, which is the cheapest option but which will not provide high sound quality. Analog multitrack recorders are good and can add a warmth that some people prefer, but they can be difficult to maintain, and the tapes can be expensive. Digital multitracks are very popular, as they can record eight tracks onto a digital tape and can be linked to each other to create 16, 24 or more tracks; most pro studios have some form of digital multitrack. They are somewhat portable as well, but also require a good deal of maintenance; Hard-disk recorders, both computer-based re-corders that run in connection with your personal computer and stand-alone recorders that do essentially the same thing within a self-contained unit, are quickly becoming an inexpensive route to follow. Hard-disk recording can be more challenging to learn, but it allows you to do things that would be difficult to accomplish in traditional recording. You can, for instance, use software to copy or move one recorded track to another section of a tune, change the time, duration and pitch of a chosen note and so forth. There seems to be a new hard-disk medium coming out every six months or so, so do your research to figure out which system works best for you and your budget.

2. **Mixer**. Mixers are basically the traffic directors for all incoming and outgoing sound. All audio input (instruments, microphones and other sound sources such as CD and tape players), your recording device and (sometimes) your computer "meet" in the mixer. Each instrument is assigned its own channel, and multitimbral synths will have even more depending on the number of outputs. There are many kinds of mixers, some quite large and expensive, but for a beginning studio, you probably won't need more than a 16-channel mixer. If you plan on recording live instruments or vocals, you'll need a mixer that can accept microphone (i.e., analog) signals. If you plan on using only MIDI and keyboard (i.e., digital) sounds, you can get away with a simple line mixer that routes all the tracks to an overall mix. All mixers have controls for volume, equalization and effects that can be applied to each input (or "track"). The various tracks are fed into the master mix, which is then sent to the recording device.

3. **Monitors**. You might think that listening to everything on headphones seems like a good idea, but it is also helpful to be able to hear your music through a set of stereo monitors as it's recorded. Monitors can tell you what the mix will sound like in a room, while headphones are most useful for listening to details in a mix. You can buy powered monitors, which have power amps built into them to amplify the sound, or you can get unpowered monitors, which require the use of an external power amp. There are differences of opinion as to which type of system sounds best, and you should decide for yourself which you prefer. Listen for clarity in the high and low ends and make sure that the sound is consistent and even throughout the entire spectrum.

4. **Sequencer**. There are many different ways to sequence your music. Sequencing is basically a form of multitracking, with the sequencer controlling most parameters for each track. When you play a MIDI keyboard into a sequencer, the sequencer captures all the notes and MIDI information, allowing it to be played back exactly as you originally played it. Sequencers can also *quantize* tracks—that is, "round off" uneven or shorter rhythmic values to a larger preset value. Sequencers allow you to edit, create and save tracks without having to dump them to a recording medium right away. Stand-alone sequencers have a portability advantage, but most studios have some kind of computer-based sequencer, often combined with a hard-disk recorder, so that a sequence can be run and recorded to a hard disk simultaneously. This is quickly becoming the standard system, and it is getting cheaper and easier to own and operate.

5. **Keyboards**. A multitimbral synth of some sort will serve you well, as you can assign different patches to different MIDI channels, giving you more sonic capability. Modules can be a cheap and easy means of adding to your sound palette, and they don't take up nearly as much space as a keyboard. Use one dedicated keyboard as your controller, i.e., the instrument through which you input information to the sequencer. This controller should be touch and velocity sensitive, and have at least 61 keys.

6. **Something to mix down to**. You'll need a DAT (digital audio tape) recorder or a CD burner to save all your mixes to a portable medium. After you've completed the recording process, you'll record all of your mixes to one of these to create a master. Choose whichever offers the best features for your needs.

7. **Miscellaneous hardware**. You will also need things like keyboard stands, racks, cables, microphone stands, etc. in your studio setup. Racks are useful for keeping your workspace neat, which will make the recording process easier and more efficient. Make sure that any gear you install in a rack is solidly mounted. Good cables are a necessity; when purchasing cables, always buy at least one extra cable of each type.

A keyboard's sound can be manipulated through the use of effects, both built-in and external (sometimes called "outboard gear"). It is worthwhile to learn everything you can about the different types of effects built into your keyboard and what they can do. This way, you can confidently program your synth's internal effects, as well as learn the art of working with effects pedals.

There are many ways to alter sound via effects. The following explanations are merely guidelines—there is nothing like experiencing them yourself and tweaking them as you play and learn.

MODULATION EFFECTS

There are many types of modulation effects, which are based on the delaying of the initial sound. Each type of effect can be mixed with a certain amount of non-delayed sound to make the effect more or less predominant.

Flanging creates a short delay that modulates the sound in a variety of ways, from a mild gurgling effect to a jet airplane "whoosh." *Phasing* is similar to flanging, but the input and output sounds get crossed, creating a phase effect. *Chorusing* provides depth by adding a short delay to simulate two instruments playing at once. *Echo* is something we're all familiar with—the (often fading) repetition of a sound at regular or irregular intervals. *Vibrato* is a slight and rapid change in pitch, the rich but subtle "wobble" you often hear in the voice of a good singer. *Tremolo* is a slight varying of the amplitude or a very rapid reiteration of a sound (think of a violinist quickly bowing back and forth on a single note), producing an effect that can be similar to vibrato. There are many offshoots of these effects, all with different names but with the same set of general parameters as those mentioned above.

Rate or *speed* here refers to the speed at which a sound is modulated. *Depth, range* or *amount* is the amount of modulation applied to the delay time—the addition of a more "effected" tone to the sound. *Balance, mix* or *blend* determines how much of the delayed/modulated sound is being output; a balance of 100% will give you all effected sound, while a balance of 0% will give you just the basic input (dry) sound. *Feedback, recirculation* or *regeneration* determines how much of the output sound feeds back into the input; the more you feed back in, the heavier the delay (think of echo effects).

All of these effects are available in rack-mountable or pedal forms. Pedals are the devices you see guitarists stepping on and tweaking during a gig. They can be very handy in a live situation when you can use the controls (rate, balance, etc.) to alter the sound at will. Rack effects aren't as easy to fiddle with on the fly, but they are very handy in the MIDI studio. Many rack-effects modules can produce several types of effects at once, such as a chorus plus a delay. They are programmable and usually MIDI-controllable. Most keyboards also come with built-in effects.

REVERB

Reverb is an electronic simulation of an acoustic space; it allows your keyboard to sound as if it were in a large room, a tight closet, a cathedral, etc. It adds depth to tracks and makes them sound more realistic. It is, in short, the most necessary element in a MIDI studio. Most rack units have some sort of reverb built in, and some are dedicated reverb units. When you can't afford to record in a great-sounding room, a dry room with reverb added can create the ambience you need and want.

There are different parameters for reverb. *Type* indicates the kind of reverb—"room," "hall," and "spring" (the classic twangy sound in much music of the 1950s) are among the most popular. *Size* is the size of the room to be emulated. It can be described in cubic meters or cubic feet, or in milliseconds. *Early reflections* are the first sets of echoes you hear, typically after 20–50 milliseconds, while larger values create the feeling of a larger space. *Pre-delay*, like early reflections, controls the time before the reverb begins. *Decay time* controls how long the reverberated sound lasts until it fades away completely. *Mix, balance* or *blend* determines how much of the reverberated sound is output, 100% being all reverberated sound, 0% all dry sound. *Gated reverb* makes the output sound as if it were backwards by using a volume threshold to determine when the sound and reverb are output. This effect has a distinctive sound which was popularized in the 1980s by Peter Gabriel, Phil Collins and many others. There are many other parameters that have different names from manufacturer to manufacturer, and some are more complicated than others. However, they will all have these basic functions.

COMPRESSORS/LIMITERS

Compressors control the peaks and valleys of a recorded piece of music. They can boost the quiet parts and tone down the louder parts to create a more even sound. They can boost the overall level of a track, adding life to an otherwise dull-sounding song, but they can also squeeze the sound into a sonic spectrum that many find unnatural. Either way, a compressor is an essential part of any studio, whether it is used a great deal or only rarely. *Limiters* act in a similar way to compressors, but they flatten all peaks (higher volume levels), leaving lower levels unchanged.

All compressors have a few basic controls. The *threshold* is the level at which the compressor kicks in. A lower threshold triggers the compression at lower levels, while a higher threshold needs a louder level to kick in. *Ratio* is the amount of output level signal change from the input sound. A higher ratio increases the effect of the compression. *Attack* determines how long it takes for the compression to kick in. Longer attack times let more of the natural input sound through without being compressed. *Output control* is the overall volume for the track. It's used to balance the input and output levels to make them equal. *Decay* is the time it takes for the compressor's sound to die away. A longer decay time sounds more natural, while a short decay creates a "whoosh" effect. The *hard knee/soft knee* controls how quickly the compression kicks in. Soft knee slowly brings in the compression once the signal has reached the threshold, while hard knee kicks in the full amount of compression once the threshold is achieved.

There are other settings on some compressors, but these are the basic controls. In general, compression is used during mixdown, where it is applied to certain tracks or to the entire mix. Guitarists and live sound mixers use it to keep the overall level from getting too loud.

So much to buy ... this can all seem a little intimidating to one's wallet, but you don't need to go all out when setting up your first studio. Pieces can be acquired one at a time, and there's no need to buy the newest and most expensive piece of gear when you can get something else that will do much the same thing for less. It's a good idea to start out with a small, basic system, since when you're first getting the hang of this, you will learn everything much more quickly from a small setup than from an overwhelming one. First learn how to get a great sound out of next to nothing, then add new gear as you go.

Here's an example of a small MIDI studio setup. Note how the different effects are routed through the mixer's auxiliary ("aux") sends—everything feeds into the mixer and, eventually, into the master recorder.

POSSIBLE MIDI STUDIO SETUP

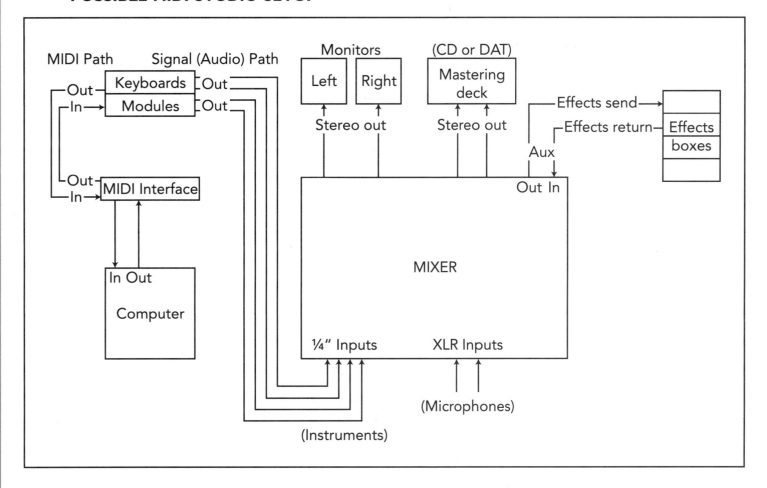

People have created home studios in closets, garages, and all sorts of other tiny spaces. If you don't have enough room in your home, you can rent a small space somewhere, but it's always a good idea to start small. If you already have a spot where your keyboard rig is set up, then you have a place. A corner makes a good place, as you will be able to get to every piece of gear easily when it is arranged around you in an "L" or "V" formation. As a rule, the gear you need to adjust most should be the most accessible, while gear that you rarely change, like power amps and reverb units, can be placed in a lower or more inaccessible location.

POSSIBLE MIDI STUDIO SETUP (IN A CORNER)

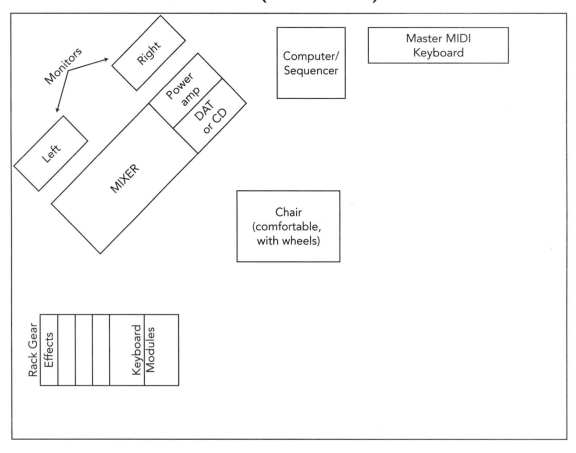

You can set up your studio in any space you see fit, but a basic principle to keep in mind is that the monitors should be facing the farthest point in the room. For example, if you have a narrow room in which to work, your monitors should be facing the far wall, not the near wall.

POSSIBLE MIDI STUDIO SETUP (NARROW ROOM)

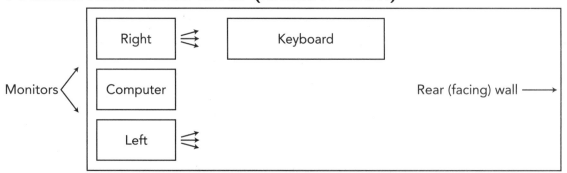

There are many other considerations in building a MIDI studio: microphones, sound reinforcement, polarity and many others. If you want more in a studio—for instance, the ability to record multiple live instruments—consult a professional or a detailed book on the subject to be sure you have all the proper elements in the proper arrangement.

Chapter 4

MAKING MONEY AS A KEYBOARD PLAYER

Fame and fortune, rock and roll. The music business is a rough line of work, and it rarely offers real financial security—but you've probably already heard that from your parents, your grandparents, uncles and aunts and just about everyone else. Most people are used to a lifestyle that contains a steady job, but the life of a professional musician is anything but steady. If your main reasons for getting into music involve visions of *Rolling Stone* covers and a Brink's truck backing up to your front door, you might want to reconsider your profession. Of course, you can play part-time while holding down a full-time job, and you won't be as hard-pressed to make a living from music. But if music is the only thing you can and want to do, and you just can't live without doing it, here are a few ways to make money with your talents as a keyboardist.

TEACHING

Anybody with some ability and knowledge can teach piano at a beginning or intermediate level. Even if you think you're not a good enough player or teacher, that may not be as important as whether you are open, friendly and communicative. Some teachers book students through a music store, and even use the store's space to give lessons. In this case the store will normally charge a flat fee or take a percentage of your earnings, but the cost to you may include useful services and benefits like bookkeeping, store discounts and so on.

You can also teach in your home or studio or, sometimes with an additional charge, at the homes of students. If you want only a few private students, put up signs or take out ads in local newspapers announcing your availability as a teacher. Be sure to include all contact information—name, address (if pertinent), telephone number and e-mail address. State how many years you have been playing, summarize your own training (including your own teachers and any degrees/certificates earned), and describe your teaching experience. You should make your ad look as professional as possible.

Your teaching doesn't need to be limited to basic piano. If you are so inclined, you can also give individual or group lessons in synthesizer basics, keyboard technique, MIDI, recording, sequencing, synth programming and so forth. The trick is to offer something that will attract multiple students. The more you know about a subject, the better. If you advertise that you are giving a master class on piano tuning but have limited knowledge or experience in that area, things will probably not go well.

ACCOMPANYING VOICE AND INSTRUMENTAL LESSONS

If you have experience playing with vocalists or instrumentalists, seek out those who need an accompanist for their lessons; private teachers, schools and college music departments can be especially helpful in this regard. This is not only a chance for you to make money, but also an opportunity to sharpen your accompanying and sight-reading skills. You should charge for both time spent with the singer or player and for the lesson itself. Usually, you will not need to be at the lesson the whole time, as the coach or teacher will supervise the warm-up.

The charge for accompanying should be less than that for a private piano lesson. Avoid putting an undue strain on the singer's or player's finances, since he or she is already paying the teacher—and reasonable fees will lead to excellent word-of-mouth advertising for your services. Ask around in your area to determine what is an appropriate amount to charge.

ACCOMPANYING DANCE AND MOVEMENT CLASSES

If you can sight-read well, go to a local dance studio and ask if they need any accompanists for their classes. Watch another accompanist in action to see how he/she follows the movement of the dancers. Accompanying dance is not always easy, and it requires a good improvisational sense and the ability to follow someone else's sense of rhythm, no matter how irregular or bad. Don't lie and say that you are familiar with tap or ballet if you aren't. Your lack of knowledge will quickly become evident, and you'll have a group of unhappy dancers on your hands. And who, aside from Bruce Lee or Jackie Chan, is more apt to be ready with a well-placed kick?

ACCOMPANYING STAGE PRODUCTIONS

Chances are, there are organizations in your area that put on plays, musicals, revues and similar productions. Whether a community theater or a bigger company, they will likely need music. If they do, they will probably need a pianist, to play for either rehearsals or performances, as a soloist or as part of an ensemble.

In the case of a play, you may be hired to play incidental music. Some directors will have particular music in mind; others will use original music (by you or others) written expressly for the production. The smaller a production is, the smaller the budget and the number of musicians will be. In high schools and colleges, there will most likely be a student band (though some include professional "ringers"), whereas a community or regional theater will assemble an ad hoc group according to the means and needs of the production. (The band enlisted for a play or musical, by the way, is often known as a "pit band.")

Whether you are playing alone or leading a band, you should be aware that beginning and intermediate (and sometimes even professional) singers may need a pitch reference (the notes they are to sing) on a regular basis. They will be onstage, while you will be in the pit, offstage or even in some more remote location. Since the singers will not always be near the instrumentalists, the accompaniment must be played as clearly as possible. At the same time, the accompaniment must never overpower the singers. It can be tricky to achieve the right balance, but rehearsals, especially in the actual performance space, should give you an idea of how loud to play.

When working in the theater, especially community theater, it is good to keep in mind that the goal is to put on the best possible show you can. Egos should not get in the way. Sometimes, miscommunications and problems unrelated to you or the music can cause friction among musicians, stage performers, the director and other theater personnel. No matter what the situation may be, always act as professionally as possible and keep in mind that the world of music can be very small. You never know when you may need to work with someone again and in what capacity. Remember: The singer or director you abuse today, no matter how much he or she may deserve it, may be the person who refuses to hire you for a more pleasant, important and lucrative gig in the future.

PLAYING IN CLUBS AND RESTAURANTS (PROVIDING BACKGROUND MUSIC)

Providing a musical backdrop in a club, restaurant or similar establishment is a good way for you, either as a solo act or as part of a band, to make money—as long you don't mind serving as atmosphere instead of being the focus of attention. Look for places that already use live music and ask the manager or owner what he/she needs to hear from you in order to hire you. Of course, your musical style should fit the site you want to play; industrial goth, for example, will generally not work well in a hotel's cocktail lounge. Most places with background music tend to use low-key jazz or other "soft" styles. Solo gigs are also an option, as some places will have only the space or budget to hire one person. Just be sure that you have your solo chops together and can play for hours at a time if called upon to do so.

If a place wants you to audition, *don't* audition during normal business hours—otherwise, the establishment is merely obtaining free entertainment. (Establishments that request this sort of audition are likely too cheap to hire anyone, anyway). If you're trying to play in a place that hasn't featured music before, check with other musicians around town to see how much other similar venues are paying; this will give you an idea of what to charge. Make sure all venues have an entertainment license, as you don't want police coming in and closing the joint (and you) down in the middle of your set—extreme as it may sound, it happens. Newer establishments usually need extra business to justify having music, so the more self-promotion you do, the better. It never hurts to have a lot of people at your gigs.

PLAYING WITH OTHER BANDS (BEING A SIDEMAN)

Keyboardists tend to be a distinctive breed of musician, perhaps because they have to handle as many as 88 keys and 10 notes at a time. For whatever reason, there usually isn't a glut of truly great keyboard players. This can be a good thing: If you are a decent player with a good rig, you can play or record with other bands as a musical hired gun.

Some bands, mostly guitar-based ones, don't use keyboards, or use them sparingly. When a band requests your services, you should charge them different fees for recording in a studio or filling out the sound on a gig. Some bands add extra instruments for important gigs, such as recording industry showcases, in order to thicken the sound. For such an event, you should do your job well and be paid accordingly, all without becoming an official member of the band. To determine an appropriate fee, ask around to find out what other keyboard professionals think is proper according to the type of job, your abilities and the geographical area in which you live and/or perform. Your local musician's union will have a list detailing different types of gigs and their scale rates.

PLAYING AT WEDDINGS, PARTIES AND OTHER EVENTS

Weddings, receptions, parties etc. can be your steadiest and most lucrative source of gigs. At such events you will generally be expected to play a large number of tunes in a wide variety of styles, from 1920s jazz to contemporary Top 40, so a good deal of prep work is necessary. A lot is expected of you, and this should be reflected in your fee.

Wedding bands differ in size and makeup, the musicians' pay, etc. Most have a leader who takes care of all booking and business aspects. Because this can be time-consuming and difficult work—filing contracts, dealing with nervous brides, coordinating schedules—leaders generally take a greater share of the money than other band members, as much as 50–100% more.

Some bands rehearse a great deal, especially to learn new tunes; others never rehearse and just depend on their members to know lots of different tunes themselves or to be excellent sight-readers. Some bands go by a name but really have no permanent members, just one or two relatively steady players. Most will have charts for many of their songs so that a new player can step in and read them at a moment's notice. Naturally, the level of musicianship has to be relatively high for this type of band.

As suggested earlier, the pay for these gigs can be substantial, but there are several things you must be aware of:

1. **You will perform all cover songs.** If you only want to play original music, a wedding band isn't the place for you.

2. **You will play for different people each time.** Generally, the majority of guests at such a function will not have heard you before. You will have to win them over and get them to appreciate your music, which is not always easy. The age range of those present may be wide, from young children to senior citizens. While it is impossible to please everyone, your mission is to please as many people as possible—which means playing many different types of music.

3. **You will encounter nervous and/or uptight clients.** Even if you're not the one booking the band, at one time or another you'll be on the receiving end of an unhappy patron's complaint. Some people involved in these situations can be very difficult to deal with, so you have to figure out how to work with them. Patience is a particular virtue here, because you want to seem professional and courteous, even if your client isn't. Deal with difficult people as best as you can without getting visibly upset. That way everyone is happy—clients get what they need, and you get paid.

4. **The work is monotonous.** The other players in a wedding band may not always be first-class, and playing the same old tunes again and again can get tedious, especially if you don't like the music to begin with. When monotony strikes at your soul, alleviate boredom by challenging yourself. Try playing a familiar song with your left hand instead of your right. Be careful that you don't commit serious gaffes during numbers that contain your personal challenges, but realize that people aren't always paying attention to you, especially during the early sets.

Stevie Wonder *was a Motown child prodigy who hit the top of the charts with* Fingertips (Part 2) *in 1963. He matured into one of the most influential artists of the 20th century, performing most of the instruments on his dazzling solo albums.*

If you decide that joining a wedding band is for you, there are some other things to keep in mind:

1. **Be prepared to make a commitment.** Some bands are amenable to their players "subbing out," while others go to pieces if even one different person is added to the mix. Ask a prospective band what they expect from you, and how many gigs and rehearsals they usually have each month. If you cannot meet their schedule, it's probably not a good situation for you.

2. **Know how your skills shape up relative to those of the band.** Listen to and observe in action any band you think you want to join. You want to make sure that the skill level and standards of the band are similar to your own. If you are not good enough, you will waste their time; if they are not good enough, they will waste yours.

3. **Find out how the band learns the music.** If you are expected to learn dozens of songs and don't have the time, a band with charts for all of their music may be a good bet.

4. **Find out how the band operates at gigs.** One way of structuring sets at a function is to play an hour-long set, break for at least 15 minutes and repeat the cycle. Note, however, that since a party can involve random or spontaneous events like toasts and speeches, sets can begin or end at any time. Some bands provide "continuous" music, which means that at least one member, if not the whole band, is playing at all times. While some people like this, the level of performance will probably suffer greatly if, for instance, a guitarist is stuck playing solo for 15 minutes. In fact, it is likely that the client will want to use your break times to play certain CDs. If a band expects you to play continuously, make sure you are getting extra money for it—it will require more work, and you should be paid accordingly.

5. **Know what a band expects of you.** If a band thinks you have an amazing array of synth sounds and will cover keyboard and horn parts, make sure you have the ability and equipment to do so. If they want you to cover two parts at once, you should either have two keyboards on the gig or have a split keyboard with one sound in the lower half and another in the upper half. In the latter case, some synth programming might be necessary.

In general, wedding bands can offer a decent income to supplement your other gigs or jobs. Being in one is a great way to learn new tunes, but the burnout factor can come into play as a result of seeing so many listless people paying no attention to your music. Know that just about every great musician out there has done at least one wedding or party gig. Most have done many more; even veteran players still take such engagements to supplement their incomes. (See Chapters 5 and 6 for more on the topics of joining, rehearsing and performing with a band.)

Being in a band may or may not provide a source of income. Most bands that play original music don't make huge sums for their gigs. However, you might be able to make some money from a recording of your music. Actually, this is a good idea whether you are with a band or perform as a solo act.

If you are doing the recording yourself—i.e., no record companies or outside investors are involved—then the process can be quite affordable, which means more money for you. CDs are becoming easier and cheaper to manufacture, and it's not unheard of to find companies or cottage industries that can make them for $2.00 each, including artwork. You have a number of options, so shop around to see which company offers the best overall price and product. The fact that someone can make your CDs for a dollar a pop doesn't guarantee that you will receive a quality product. If you need fewer than 100 CDs with no fancy package, it's generally worthwhile to make your own using a CD burner (either a computer-driven or a stand-alone unit). This is a practical route whether you are using the CD as a demo or just testing the musical waters.

You can mark up the price of your CD to reflect how much you spent to create it in terms of time, materials, gear, etc. Self-produced CDs sell for about $10.00 to $15.00 each. Pricing a CD too high might stop people from buying it, while pricing it too low will cheapen the product and add less to your wallet. Settle on a happy medium.

While you may not realize a serious profit from your CD, you can, with effort and diligence, expect to break even. Keep in mind that a recording is an investment in yourself (and/or your band) and your music. If you believe in the music you make and the product you put out, the financial gain from your talent and hard work can be particularly rewarding.

PHOTO • LYDIA CRISS/COURTESY OF STAR FILE PHOTO, INC

Billy Joel, one of the most popular keyboard players in the world, became a recording artist for Columbia Records in the 1970s. His tour with superstar pianist Elton John was a piano aficionado's dream come true.

Chapter 5

HOW TO GET INTO A BAND

If you're ready to join a band, you're already well on the way if you can play your instrument with a relatively high degree of skill—and have good hygiene, control of your ego and a positive attitude! If you're fairly new to the music scene, look for bands or musical projects whose members are on roughly the same musical level as, or are slightly better than, you. You'll find that playing with musicians better than you will make you play better as well, and that with them you will be able to do things you didn't think you were capable of. However, being in a band whose abilities are markedly better than yours may cause problems, as one lesser musician can disrupt the entire musical flow of the entire group. In other words, aim high, but not too high.

The role of a keyboard player in bands playing in most contemporary styles does not necessarily require you to be a virtuoso on the keys. Technical wizardry is often the province of other instruments, allowing you to add subtle colors and textures. We'll explore this concept more fully in later chapters.

Here are some ways to get into a band:

1. **Ask your friends.** Seek out friends and acquaintances who are in bands. Put the word out that you are looking for a group situation—you will probably get calls to come and play with a group, or even with just one person with an idea for a band. Having a personal connection is a great advantage. Any sort of recommendation is valuable, especially if you're entering into to a situation about which you know very little.

2. **Scour audition ads.** Look in your local paper—weeklies are usually best—or in music stores for ads placed by bands in search of members. There are always bands looking for someone to join them, either because a member has left, they're still in the process of formation, or they've just decided to add keyboards to their lineup. You can also use the Internet to look for band postings in your area—many on-line music sites have classified ads that should prove helpful.

3. **Do it yourself.** If you have an idea or concept for a band, there's nothing wrong with getting it off the ground on your own. Place an ad in a local paper or ask around. Make clear your intentions for the proposed band, your musical influences and the fact that you're just starting out. It's pointless and detrimental to make false claims—that you have gigs already lined up or that your uncle is a big-shot producer. Even if you *do* have a producer for an uncle, it's btter to keep that out of the ad and to keep the focus on the band itself. That way, you'll find people more committed to a start-up project. Remember: You don't necessarily have to be the leader of the group, even if the group is your idea. Ideally a band should be a democratic union in which everyone has an equal say in what the group does.

Chances are, you've auditioned for something in your life, whether for a spot on a Little League team or a role in a play. Whatever the situation, you were being judged. Some people have a hard time with this, saying that they don't like to be judged or compared to others, but we judge and compare things every day, from the people we like to the toothpaste we don't. The process of finding the right person for a job—or a band—isn't necessarily unfair; it's just a part of existence.

SETTING UP AN AUDITION

Most groups auditioning prospective members will want to know specifically about your qualifications to determine whether you're worthy to be in their band. Some will just want to talk to you to see if you're on the same page, musically speaking. Likewise, your first contact with a band or one of its members will be an important factor in helping you decide whether or not you actually want to audition. Be especially attentive and observant, and don't be afraid to ask questions, whether about the band's musical style and goals or about practical issues like equipment, schedules and personnel.

A band in search of a new member should be forthcoming, though not mindlessly boastful, about its background and accomplishments. Be wary of a band that tells you how great their music is but doesn't want you to hear it. At the same time, realize that sometimes band members are suspicious that new people may steal the group's songs.

The band's members will want to get a good idea of what you are like—not only as a musician, but as a person. Half of a band's musical chemistry comes from the personal chemistry among the members. It's best to be truthful, and at the same time not to brag. Don't say that you've traveled around the world and played for thousands of people if you haven't. Even if you have done those things, you don't necessarily need to trumpet them, at least not right away. You can always share more of your background—and amusing anecdotes—*after* you get the gig.

Some bands will ask what you look like, your age and other personal questions. They are likely interested in how you will fit in with the band's image. Despite all you hear about horrible, messy band breakups, many groups, both famous and obscure, have existed for years (even decades) because they have worked well together on several levels. Discovering as much about prospective members as possible is obviously a band's key to finding—and keeping—good, valuable personnel.

GETTING READY FOR AN AUDITION

Let's say you've been given a time slot to audition with the band, or at least some of its members. If the band has given you a recording of their music to study, learn it as thoroughly as possible. If the band has a vocalist, it's a good idea to know the lyrics at key points (e.g., the last line before the chorus or any other spot that will cue a transition), especially if you have to change sounds or get ready for a more complicated part. Knowing the lyrics also earns you brownie points from the lyricist, since so many of them claim that nobody pays attention to lyrics these days.

Before you leave home, make sure all of your gear is in good working order and that you have everything you need. It's a drag to ask a stranger for a spare cable, and it mars your image as a professional. Arrive at the audition at least 15 minutes early. If you are bringing your own equipment, such as keyboards and amplification, set up whatever you can beforehand. The less time you take to get ready in the audition itself, the more time you will have to play.

DURING THE AUDITION

If you have any questions about chords or forms in a tune, ask the band before you play. When you run through the songs for the first time, listen carefully, as the music may differ from how it sounds in the recording. Ask about this, and they will most probably be happy to explain—and will appreciate your attentive ear. You can be sure that in every case, playing the songs live will feel different from playing with the recording. Play with confidence, not too loudly and not too quietly. Be sincerely apologetic about anything you may not know or any mistakes you may make, but avoid saying "I'm sorry" repeatedly. If you later find out that you didn't get the gig for one reason or another, politely ask one or more of the members why—you may gain insight into what to do differently at your next audition. If you don't get the gig, learn from the experience—and realize that the more you audition, the more comfortable you'll feel doing it.

PHOTO • LYDIA CRISS/COURTESY OF STAR FILE PHOTO, INC

Earl "Bud" Powell, *an important bebop innovator, set the standard for modern jazz keyboard soloing in the 1940s.*

Chapter 6

REHEARSAL TIPS

What do you do once you've made it into a band or put together one of your own? Let's assume you have all the musical slots filled: guitar, bass, drums, vocals (in some cases) and of course keyboards. You need a place to rehearse. What are your options?

WHERE TO REHEARSE WITH YOUR BAND

1. **A garage (or basement, etc.).** Make no mistake: Great bands have been born in garage rehearsal spaces. Classic tracks like The Kingsmen's *Louie, Louie* were recorded in a garage; some just sound as though they were. One of the great advantages of a rehearsal space like this is that it's generally free. One drawback, however, is that most garages were built to store cars, lawnmowers and tools—not for optimum acoustic value. Still, the relative isolation of a garage may go far in alleviating one important problem you may encounter elsewhere: disturbing others with your rehearsals. Of course, neighbors will appreciate your consideration when it comes to volume levels and the time of day you rehearse.

   In a garage rehearsal situation you will have to furnish some sort of amplification for anyone who might need it. Vocalists sound best amplified through a PA or similar system rather than through a cheap guitar amp. The better everyone can hear everyone else, the better the rehearsal will be.

   Some basements will make an excellent place to rehearse, provided that they are dry, uncluttered (allowing you plenty of space), and that whoever lives above doesn't mind the noise (or isn't home).

2. **A rehearsal studio.** Most areas of the country have rehearsal studios that musicians can rent; look for ads in the phone book or in local newspapers with good music coverage. Both hourly and monthly rentals are generally available. In the case of hourly rentals, there will generally be some kind of sound system in the room, along with a drum set and amps for bass and guitar players. Not all studios will have these elements, so call around to see what is available.

   Rental studios range from foul-smelling, postage stamp–sized dumps to beautiful, great-sounding places that are nice enough to live in. Rates will vary according to location, size, and amenities. Be aware that a space that seems like a deal may not be at all suitable for your needs. Check out a studio ahead of time, paying close attention to factors like soundproofing, cleanliness and air quality—all of these can have a direct impact on your rehearsals. Try to hear another band rehearse in the same space, and listen for sounds bleeding in from other rooms. If you can't look at a particular studio ahead of time, ask around to find out if anyone you know has rehearsed there before. A solid recommendation from someone you trust is the next best thing to seeing it for yourself.

If your band is really serious about rehearsing two or three times a week, it can be a good idea to go in together on a space that is yours alone. With space that is exclusive, you can rehearse at any time, customize it according to your needs and tastes, and use it to store your instruments and equipment. You will of course have to supply your own amps, sound system, etc., but you will save money in the long run compared to the cost of hourly studio rentals. Keep in mind that you may want to be sure that the band will work out before investing time and money in a place of your own, so an hourly space may be a good bet as you start out.

PHOTO • BILL GREENSMITH/COURTESY OF STAR FILE PHOTO, INC

Major "Big Maceo" Merriweather *came up during the boogie-woogie craze and went on to become one of the most popular blues artists on the Chicago scene in the 1940s. His piano style was hugely influential to the young pianists coming up in Chicago, most notably two of Muddy Waters's pianists: Little Johnny Jones and Otis Spann.*

Merriweather both sang and played, and his songs were mainly his own, many of them in the sixteen-bar blues form. His best-known song is Worried Life Blues, *which borrows a verse from guitarist Sleepy John Estes. Merriweather's first recording session took place in 1941, and unfortunately, his last was in 1945. Shortly after that time, he suffered a paralyzing stroke, and though he recovered from it, his playing never reached its previous level. The 1945 session produced Merriweather's solo masterpiece,* Chicago Breakdown, *a classic example of boogie-woogie piano at its finest.*

Most club owners and bookers will want to hear some sort of recording of your band before they book you. With the price of manufacturing CDs continuing to drop, it is becoming easier and more economical to produce a recording of your own. CDs are also the best medium for the listener, as it is simple to skip from track to track, and the sound quality is superior to that of an audio cassette. Most people who book venues won't have time to listen to a demo recording all the way through, so here are some guidelines to ensure that your music will be heard and appreciated:

1. **Don't go overboard.** A band's first demo need not be a full studio recording. One easy way to record your band is to set up two identical microphones in front of the group. Position the mikes at ear level and about as far apart from one another as your own ears to capture the sound close to the way one would hear it in person.

   Place the amps and instruments at equal distances from the microphones and record the band playing through one song. Listen to the playback to judge the overall balance and clarity. Reposition the players or microphones as needed.

2. **Don't include too many songs.** When you've finished recording all the band's songs, pick the three or four that sound best. A demo should be a sonic résumé, an encapsulation of the band's style, sound and skills. It's a good idea to make the first track a quick, attention-getting song—your best one, if possible. This will grab the listener's attention and make him/her want to listen to more. Place slower, more lyrical songs in the middle, and end the demo on a high note with another upbeat, ear-catching number. Take the listener on a trip through your band's sound.

3. **Edit carefully.** You don't want the listener to hear comments made between takes, so leave ample silence both before and after each track as you record. This will make it easier to edit the recording and to burn CDs or cassettes. Leave about three to four seconds between songs on the final master. This will give the listener time to prepare for the next tune.

4. **Present an attractive product.** There's no greater turn-off to a booker or agent than a recording that looks cheap or cheesy. With the availability of so many desktop graphics programs, a sharp-looking cover is easy to make and good for your image. A photograph of the band, the higher the quality the better, is also beneficial. If you submit cassettes, be sure to use new blanks for optimal sound quality and appearance. The demo doesn't have to be shrink-wrapped or even in a CD jewel case, but the better your band looks, the more positive and professional an impact you'll make.

Make sure the demo *really* captures your band—it should feel and sound like a good recording of your band playing live. The entire package should present the band as it really is. A band trying to make itself seem "bigger" than it really is is usually easy to spot, and a shoddily produced demo with poor production and graphics gives the game away even faster.

GETTING GIGS FOR THE BAND

Assuming you've got the band together and have at least 45 minutes' worth of music to play, you're ready to start gigging. Now the question is, "How do we get gigs?" You've probably already seen other bands perform in clubs or other venues. If you haven't, go now! This is the best way to know who's out there and what they're playing. Look for bands that seem to have a musical approach similar to yours and meet them if you can. Often, a recommendation to a club from another band will help you get gigs.

Once you've heard other bands and become familar with a number of venues, you should have a pretty good idea of the kind of club where your music would fit in. When you discover a place you particularly like, find out who handles entertainment bookings there and deal with him or her directly. You should have the attitude of a professional when you approach the person in charge. Have all necessary information (availability, etc.) at the ready, ask thoughtful, pertinent questions and be prepared to succinctly describe the band's style and performance experience.

So you've got a gig. Now what do you do? First, make sure that the whole band can actually make the gig. It's a real drag, not to mention a poor reflection on the band, to cancel any engagement, no matter what the circumstances. One near-certain result of a cancellation is that you'll be less likely to be booked at a venue again. Once it is clear that everyone can make the gig, how do you ensure that everything is ready? Here are a few pointers:

1. **Assemble a tight, cohesive set.** The club will let you know exactly how much time you have to perform. For a typical club gig of 45 minutes, you can assume that around 10 songs will cover the time allotted. Make a set list. Start with something that grabs people's attention, something that isn't terribly slow. As a rule, never play two slow songs in a row, or more than two songs that are in the same key or are similar in style or tempo. Your last song should be powerful and catchy so that when people leave, the sound of it will remain in their ears.

    In your last rehearsal before the gig, play your set list in order and carefully time the total length, making sure that it is no longer than the time allowed for your set. Many clubs are very strict about time limits, and some are downright rude if you exceed your allotted time. If anything, make your set shorter than the time allowed; that way, you'll have time to play everything if a guitarist's string breaks or some other unexpected situation arises. If there is time left at the end, you can always fit in an extra song or two. Have an encore prepared just in case, but don't always expect to perform it; time constraints or audience apathy may dictate a quick exit.

2. **Make sure your equipment is in good working order.** Whether or not you're able to have a sound check (which will not be possible at some clubs), make sure beforehand that all of your cables, disks, keyboards, amplifiers, etc. are in proper working order. Do a complete "idiot check" of your gear before you leave for the gig. Know exactly what you will need, including how many cables. It's better to bring too much equipment than too little. Don't take a chance on iffy gear. If a cable doesn't appear to be working well, leave it at home and buy a new one.

3. **Don't be nervous. Don't be cocky.** It's natural that you'll be nervous to some degree, especially at your first gigs, but try not to show it onstage. Channel your nervous energy into the performance. One sure cure (or at least effective treatment) for nervousness is thorough preparation. Make sure you feel good about all the music you are to play before you go onstage. Conversely, too much ego onstage will seem like a self-tribute, and most people, especially those in the record business, will see right through it. Stage presence is great, but contrived theatrics usually come off as unprofessional and ill-conceived.

4. **Be on time.** "On time" usually means being at the gig at least 30 minutes before you are to begin playing. This gives you enough time to make sure everything is ready: the setup, set list, etc. This will also ensure that you'll feel comfortable with your surroundings during the gig. Note that some places will want you there even earlier for a sound check, which is something you'll want to take advantage of. You'll be able to set up your equipment before the gig, perform the sound check and be able to leave most of the setup in place for the actual performance.

WARMING UP BEFORE A GIG

If you're lucky enough to have access to your keyboard before your gig, exercises like those below will help you warm up, play your best and keep your technique up to snuff—even if your keyboard is unplugged.

Start with the right hand and play this example slowly, moving each finger from the joint that connects hand to finger.

Now play with the left hand, using the same technique.

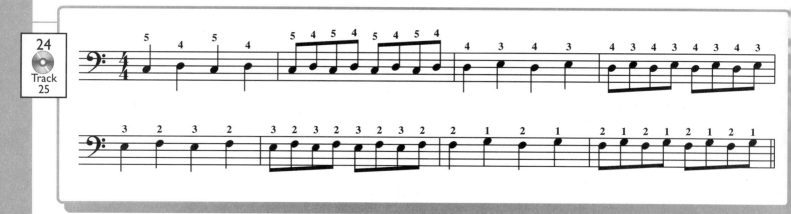

At all times, make sure that your arms are relaxed and supported all the way from your back—that is, your shoulders should support the weight of your arms, and your back should support your shoulders.

If you don't have access to your keyboard before the gig, try these other techniques for limbering up:

1. **Touch your toes (or at least try to).** Bend down slowly without bouncing on your feet. This will stretch your whole body, particularly the legs and back. Stretch your arms to their full length to ease the stiffness in those muscles.

2. **Rotate your arms.** Rotate each of your arms in an arc, supporting all movements from your back. Keep your elbows still, and move your arms from the shoulder and the back. This will ease any tension in the top of each shoulder, a frequent problem area for keyboardists.

3. **Rotate your fingers.** Slowly rotate each finger in a circle, controlling each finger from the metacarpal joint (where the finger joins the hand). Do this one finger at a time, both clockwise and counterclockwise. This warm-up is particularly effective for strengthening the joints.

4. **Pretend you're at a keyboard.** You can always pretend that you're at a keyboard when one isn't handy. Practice scales or other musical passages on a clean, flat surface. This strengthening and limbering exercise is also good for working out tricky fingerings.

By far, the best warm-up is to be relaxed and in a lucid state of mind. Of course, you shouldn't be relaxed to the point of sleepiness. Likewise, you shouldn't be too hyped up, as unchanneled excess energy can cause you to lose concentration or otherwise ruin a performance. When you're onstage, your mind should be focused on the music and nothing else. This doesn't always work in practice, but it's a good goal to keep in sight.

PHOTO • BILL GREENSMITH/COURTESY OF STAR FILE PHOTO, INC

*Virtuoso pianist **Erroll Garner**, composer of the jazz standard* Misty, *became immensely popular in the 1950s.*

RELAXING BEFORE A GIG

Everyone has a different way of getting ready for a gig. Some people like to do aerobic exercises (running, jumping jacks, push-ups, etc.) just before going onstage. This kind of workout can be great for releasing tension and getting your blood flowing. It's recommended that you don't exercise too much, however, as you don't want to tire yourself out. A maximum of 10 minutes of exercise is a good amount. Don't forget to allot an extra few minutes afterward to catch your breath, dry off, and call Mom before the gig.

Some people prefer a calmer approach to getting ready for a performance. Deep breathing is an excellent way to settle down mentally and pump more oxygen into your brain. Sit down, close your eyes and slowly inhale a deep breath as you silently count to five. Exhale slowly over the same count. Repeat this at least five times. This is an excellent way to achieve focus and calm pre-gig jitters.

If the venue allows it, you might also want to burn candles or incense if you like these. The sense of smell is a keen one, and soothing aromatherapy can be great for concentration. Keep this sort of activity to yourself in a private space, as other musicians (especially vocalists) may not appreciate the smells and smoke.

BEING ONSTAGE

There are many ways of presenting yourself onstage, most of which are determined by the type of music you play. One general, common-sense rule is to not insult the audience (though this can work well for punk shows and other scenes where rude behavior is part of the fun). You never know who is out there listening to and liking your music. Someone could be your biggest fan, but when the lead singer tells the audience how fat this person is, it usually doesn't go over well. Club owners will not generally appreciate this sort of behavior, either.

Most clubs exist for the sake of making money. The music is important, but if the band is acting obnoxious and driving patrons away, money is being lost. Clubs will get rid of bands that don't bring in (or continue to bring in) paying customers.

Try not to take more than a few seconds between each song, except in the case of, say, a band introduction or an explanation of a tune. Empty space is dull space. People will lose interest if you take a minute between each song. Talking to the crowd is fine, as it lets them know that you aren't just playing for your own amusement. Bring the audience into the music by introducing the members of the band, telling the audience the names of each song (either before or after you play it), and letting them know if you have any products for sale (demo tapes, t-shirts, temporary tattoos, etc.). Say the band's name several times in the course of the set so it will be remembered.

Above all, play the music like you mean it. Just getting on a stage in front of people can be a rush. Use that energy to play the best that you can. Many people feel completely different onstage from how they feel in real life. There is nothing wrong with this, as it can create a stage persona—something that can work well for the band if your singer stutters in real life, but onstage sings as though possessed.

AFTER THE GIG

If you can, try to grab at least a few minutes backstage or elsewhere immediately afterward to catch your breath and decompress. Right after a good hour onstage, you're probably not going to be ready to speak to anyone. If nothing else, try to at least take a few deep breaths before talking to anyone outside of the band. A good "band hang" for even a minute after the gig allows you all to figure out what worked and what didn't, and gets you ready to face the crowd again. Small talk among you and your band mates readies all of you to talk to people in the crowd.

By the way, there are two things that nobody wants to hear from you after you get off the stage: "I was great" and "I was lousy." You've perhaps moved your fans during the gig—they may think you're wonderful—but you'll spoil the mood (and shrink your fan base) by making either one of these statements, or any others that resemble them in tone. Instead, when someone comments favorably on your playing, the best thing to say is simply "thank you." Receive compliments in a humble manner, but not so humbly that you leave the impression that you feel miserable about your performance. Most people don't know what to do when a musician they just saw on stage says he wants to kill himself because of the way he played. You might feel that way, but it's generally not a good thing to communicate that to your audience.

PHOTO • LYDIA CRISS/COURTESY OF STAR FILE PHOTO, INC

Otis Spann is considered by many to be the greatest blues ensemble pianist ever. In 1952 he was introduced to Muddy Waters by Len Chess and joined Muddy in what would become a history-making band. Spann's solid, powerful playing style was derived in large part from Maceo Merriweather, who preceded him on the the Chicago scene. Spann's unique contribution to the art was in finding the perfect way to make his bold sounds enhance but never intrude upon the new sounds of Chicago blues.

Chapter 7

RECORDING IN A STUDIO

The recording studio is where you can really put your musical ideas together. Most recording studios have multitrack capabilities—that is, they can record one or more instruments at a time and give each instrument its own track. This allows them (or you) to mix the different tracks and even add more tracks if you desire. Multitracking gives you seemingly unlimited options for recording your ideas. For instance, if you don't like a take of a piano part you recorded, you can erase it and record a new one on top of the pre-existing tracks.

So, what is there to know about the recording studio?

BOOKING THE STUDIO

1. **Know the studio.** Don't book time at a studio without seeing the place first. At the very least, get a good recommendation plus a description from a friend or someone you trust.

2. **Ask questions about the studio.** Find out what they record to (analog tape, digital audio tape, computer hard disk), and how many tracks are possible. Tracks usually come in groups of eight: 8, 16, 24, 32, etc. Find out how many recording studios a facility has. Most will have at least one or two large rooms plus one or two isolation booths. If you need an acoustic piano, ask if they have one and if it will be tuned for your studio time.

3. **Find out exactly how much it will cost.** Most studios charge an hourly rate, but some will charge slightly less if you reserve large chunks of time. They'll give you a day rate, meaning that you pay a flat fee and can work in the studio as long as you want to all day, within reason. In all cases the studio will charge extra to provide tape, no matter what kind of tape it is. Some studios mark up the price substantially, so it's often best to bring your own—just make sure it's the right kind. In addition, studios may charge taxes, which may not be included in the initial fee quote. Find out the total price before you decide to book.

4. **Make sure you book time consecutively.** If you book two or more days in a row, make sure that no one else is coming in to record between your time slots, as you will have to tear down all your gear and set it up again after they finish. This can really eat into your studio time and cost both money and energy. It can take quite a while after setup is finished to get the sound levels ready for each track, so you want to do it only once.

5. **Know your engineer.** The engineer is the person who does all of the recording, mixing and tweaking of sounds; sometimes he or she also owns the studio. It's a good idea to meet your engineer before you record to discuss what you'll be recording and whether or not the person will be right for it. You probably don't want a heavy metal engineer to do a jazz record, and vice versa. The engineer will have to know the studio and its gear inside and out, have good ears and be receptive to your ideas. An engineer that rejects every one of your sonic ideas is not the right engineer. You will want someone who understands the music and is respectful; in turn, you should respect the engineer's abilities and opinions, even if they don't always coincide with yours. Good communication between an artist and an engineer is an essential element in a good recording.

A producer, in the general sense of the term, is someone who oversees the recording, providing suggestions both musically and sonically as well as a healthy atmosphere in order to get the best possible result. In other words, a producer has to be a person of many talents. If you are making your first recording, either as a solo artist or with a band, you may not want or need a producer. If you just want to document your songs, a producer is probably unnecessary, but if you have doubts about some of your music, or feel that an outside opinion would be helpful, a producer is a good thing to have.

What should a producer be and do?

1. **A producer should be genuinely interested in your music.** He or she shouldn't go so far as to co-write songs with you (unless that feels right to you) but should give helpful hints throughout the rehearsal and recording process. The producer should understand what you are trying to do musically.

2. **A producer should offer advice without demanding that you follow it.** Unless you are entirely lost, you will have some idea of what you want your music to sound like. A producer should respect your opinions but should also give you input regarding arrangements, improvisation, vocal stylings and so forth. He or she should also be able to explain why a suggestion or idea is valid.

3. **A producer should not ask for too much money.** If you are paying for the recording yourself, a producer's fee can be an important budgetary factor. This amount generally shouldn't be more than what you are paying for the studio. If the price seems a little steep, ask around and get opinions about this person, or see if there is someone else available in your price range. When it comes to recording your music, you want the best sound you can get. Sometimes it will cost more than you really want to spend, but in the end, the expense may be well worth it.

4. **A producer should be a nice person.** While you don't want someone who will agree with everything you say, you do want someone who can communicate his or her ideas clearly, effectively and with enough tact so that no egos get bruised. Music is a very personal thing, so egos can get in the way if the musicians are feeling that they're being told what to do.

How do you find a producer? For starters, there's always yourself or another band member. Record your music live, either at a gig or at a rehearsal, and listen to the recording carefully. You should listen not only to yourself closely, but to everyone else as well, since you can't always pay attention to what they are doing while you are playing. This detachment from the performance situation helps you to hear the music more clearly. If you want to use someone else, seek out a professional producer or use a friend with musical sense and trustworthy opinions. Often, a producer is present only at major recording sessions and may not be necessary for a small project. Still, another set of critical ears is almost always helpful.

Whether or not you have a producer with you in the studio, there are some things that will help you work better in the studio environment. These will save you time, energy and money. If you're paying for the studio time yourself, you will want to make every minute count. Here are some ideas:

1. **Be as prepared as possible before going into the studio.** Each musician involved in a recording should have a good idea of what he or she is going to play on a given tune. This holds true in rock, pop, R&B and other contemporary styles more so than in jazz and other more improvised forms. The more comfortable everyone is with the music, the easier it will be to record it. If you are paying for the studio, have the money ready; some people even like to pay up front so they don't have to worry about it later. Make sure you have enough recording tape, plus money for any extras that might be necessary during the recording—food, coffee, etc.

2. **Be relaxed and on time.** If you show up to the studio a little early, you will have time to relax a bit and set up whatever you need. Again, being musically prepared helps, and if you are comfortable with yourself, the music and the studio, the recording process will go much more smoothly. It also helps to get a good night's sleep the night before so you will feel rested and alert.

3. **Get a good sound in your headphones and on tape.** Some musicians overlook the need for a good monitor mix in the headphones (assuming you are using headphones) while recording. Generally, the better the sound you hear, the better you will play. A $5,000 keyboard that sounds great in the control room but lousy in your headphones won't make you feel as though you're playing a $5,000 part. Take the time to get a decent sound and mix between you and all the other instruments.

4. **Take an occasional break.** During the session, you may worry that the clock is ticking and that every minute not spent recording is a waste of time. The reality is that people, even musicians, need a break from time to time to refresh their minds and relax. A break of 15 minutes every two hours is not too much to take. If you are recording over the course of a whole day, try to take your longest break at lunchtime or dinnertime—this will save time, as everyone needs to eat at some point. You shouldn't take a break if the band is feeling ready to go and could record more tunes. Make use of inspiration and energy when you have it. Between tunes, ask the others involved how they feel. If the consensus is that they are a little tired, take a break.

5. **Bring whatever inspires you to be more creative.** This does not include animals or large objects. If you have a picture or painting you really like, it doesn't hurt to bring it along for inspiration. Some people like to burn candles and incense to make them feel more creative, but check with the studio and other musicians to make sure that it's acceptable to do this. Unless you feel confident otherwise, you probably shouldn't bring your girlfriend, boyfriend, mother, or anyone outside else outside the band. Nonessential personnel greatly increase the potential for distraction from the work at hand.

There are two ways to record: live to two-track and multitrack. Live to two-track is just that, a live recording of the band or musician to two tracks of a tape with no room for overdubbing. This is more common in classical and jazz recording sessions, in which a performance is often captured as a whole. Multitracking, as stated earlier, allows you to record one or more tracks at a time, and then to add more tracks until you have everything you need (or until there are no more tracks available). Engineers who record live to two-track tend to be very adept at getting the proper sound going to tape, levels and all, since there is no way to change it later. The mixing is really done before the recording, with only a little subtle tweaking performed during the recording. Multitracking allows for greater flexibility, but it can also take up more time and tape, and a separate mixing session will be necessary. Overall, however, multitrack sessions are more common and offer more options in terms of mixing.

When you are multitracking, there are some things to keep in mind:

1. **There may be sound from other instruments on your track.** If you are recording a separate keyboard track (i.e., the band or rhythm tracks are already down), you will be able to redo a track as much as you like until you or the engineer can't think anymore (or until you run out of money or studio time). However, if you are recording live in a room with other musicians, any sound you produce in the room may bleed through to other microphones and onto other tracks, and other sounds can likewise bleed onto your tracks. In these situations, play as well as you can. If you make mistakes, all of the live tracks may have to be redone.

2. **You can always do it again.** If you record your track to a MIDI sequencer or have a pre-recorded track, you have the freedom to come up with better ideas as you record. Many solos and parts have been created from combining different takes of the same track. This is sometimes called "comping." If you like bars 1 through 5 of your solo, but not bars 6 through 8, you can comp the two tracks together to form one track, as long as there is enough space between the two separate tracks to punch in and out of record mode. The studio allows you to take your time to find inspiration in coming up with new parts and solos. However, a track or song can become lifeless if it is played with more precision than passion. Look for perfection in imperfection.

3. **People play differently in a studio.** No matter how good the sound is in your headphones, it won't sound like your rehearsal space or the last gig. It takes time and experience to adjust to the studio environment. It can be hard to react naturally to music when it doesn't sound or feel the same as in a different setting. The best thing to do is to know what you're doing as best you can—then, anything different in the sound will be easier to address. Of course, you'll still think more about the sound than the music, but the notes will be thoroughly under your fingers.

4. **Put as much energy into your tracks as possible.** The studio process can sometimes suck the life out of your playing, particularly if the engineer isn't recording you as well as you hoped. By putting more energy into your parts (especially your solos), you can add a presence that's (hopefully) in your live playing. The natural tendency in the studio is to tighten up your playing and be more careful, but this does not have to be the case if you feel comfortable. Play hard.

Chapter 8

As a working keyboard player, it's good to be familiar with a lot of different styles of music and how the keyboard functions within them. These examples provide only a sampling, and they are by no means an attempt to encapsulate a definitive take on each style. Each style has its own way of phrasing and grooving; in playing a jazz phrase and a straight-ahead rock phrase, you will not feel and play eighth notes in the same way. You can master these differences only by listening to the music and studying the keyboard parts in depth. These examples will give you some idea of what a keyboard player's role is in various styles and will help you out if you're ever thrust into a new musical situation.

STRAIGHT-AHEAD ROCK STYLES

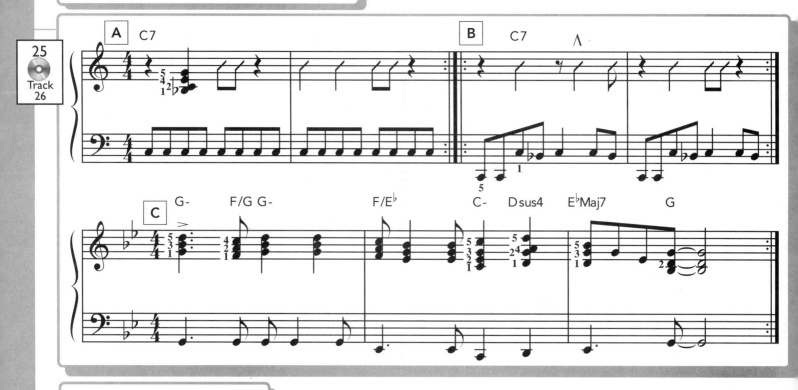

POP/BALLAD STYLES

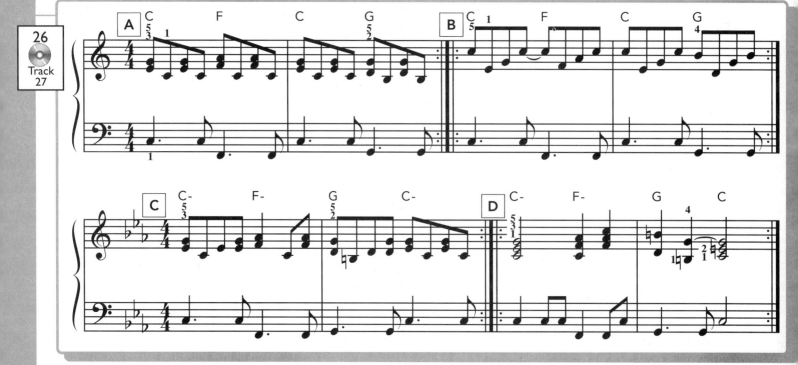

JAZZ STYLES: WALKING BASS

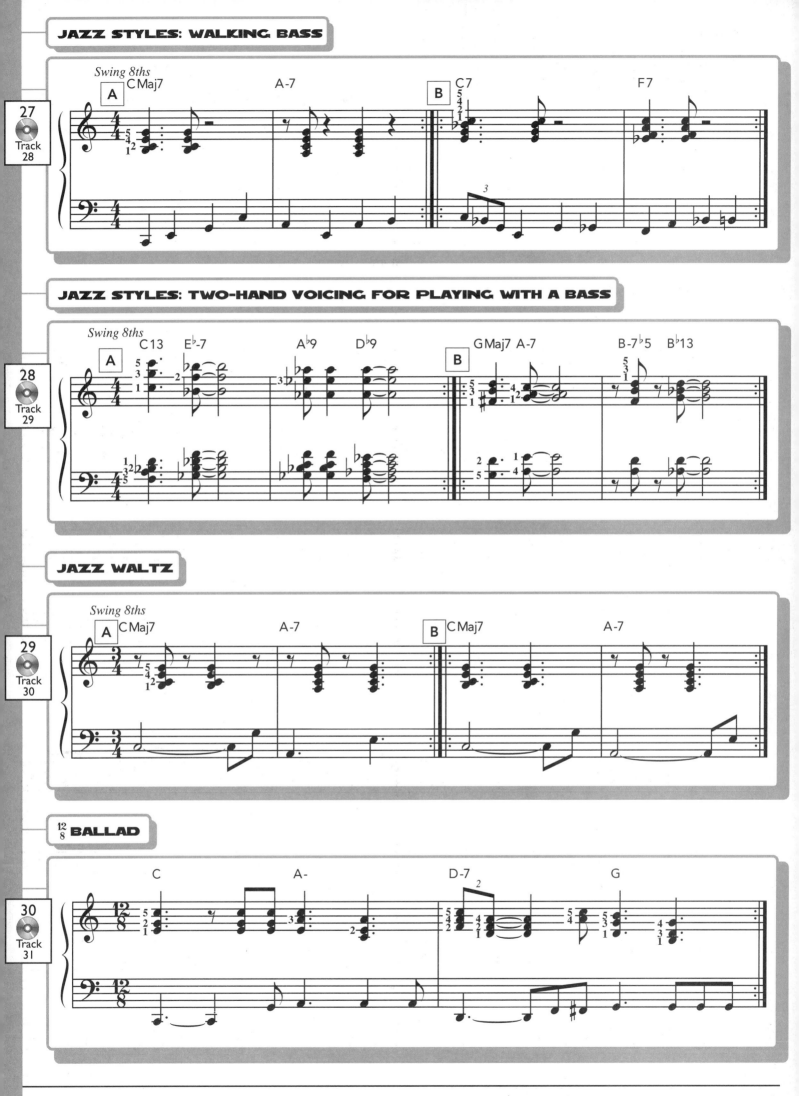

JAZZ STYLES: TWO-HAND VOICING FOR PLAYING WITH A BASS

JAZZ WALTZ

$\frac{12}{8}$ BALLAD

LATIN STYLES: SALSA, CHA-CHA, MAMBO, ETC.

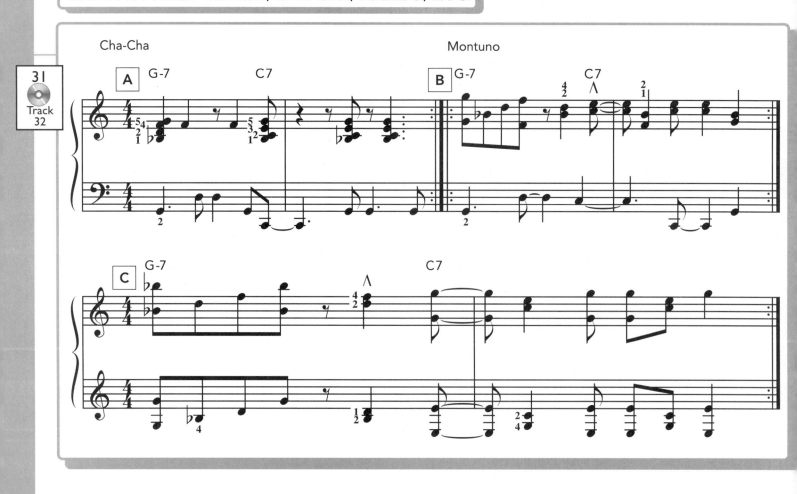

LATIN STYLES: BRAZILIAN SAMBA AND BOSSA NOVA

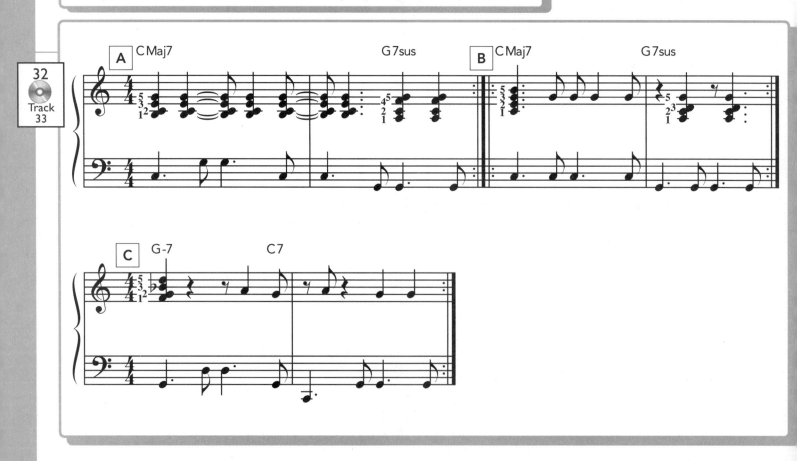

FUNKY AND SYNCOPATED PARTS FOR BOTH HANDS

FOR USE WITH STRING-LIKE PADS

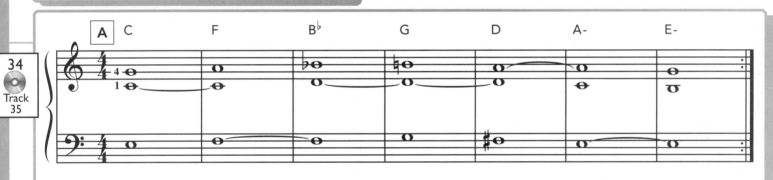

ROLLING 6/8 FEEL

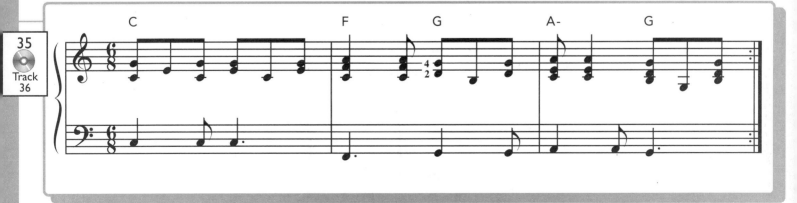

Chapter 9

There are certain songs in every style of music that are so well known that they have become "standards." This term can apply to just about any song that has been around for some time, has been recorded by more than one artist, and gets a good deal of both live and recorded play. If you hear it as an instrumental in an elevator or a supermarket, it's *definitely* a standard. Many times, it's the kind of melody that gets into your head against your will and won't go away.

The "classic" standards—the songs most closely associated with the term—date roughly from 1920 to 1955. Many standards of this period were directly influenced by artistic, cultural and technological developments that emerged in parallel: the Broadway musical, jazz, "talkies" and a number of advances in sound recording. Harold Arlen, Irving Berlin, Hoagy Carmichael, Duke Ellington, George and Ira Gershwin, Oscar Hammerstein II, E.Y. "Yip" Harburg, Lorenz Hart, Cole Porter and Richard Rodgers are just a few of the composers and lyricists who produced the core standars of this era. You might think that a song written in 1925 would sound corny today, but most standards have stood the test of time and can be remolded in many different musical styles.

CLASSIC STANDARDS

Here are some "classic" standards that are good for a keyboardist to know. This is by no means an exhaustive list, but these are songs familiar to every seasoned musician. These will give you a good place to start, and you can be sure that none will disappoint if played well.

Ain't Misbehavin'	The Lady Is a Tramp
All of Me	Lover Man
All of You	The Man I Love
All the Things You Are	Misty
Alone Together	My Funny Valentine
As Time Goes By	Night and Day
At Last	On a Clear Day
Autumn Leaves	Our Love Is Here to Stay
Bewitched	Secret Love
Body and Soul	Since I Fell for You
But Not for Me	Softly, as in a Morning Sunrise
Come Rain or Come Shine	Someday My Prince Will Come
The Days of Wine and Roses	Someone to Watch Over Me
Don't Get Around Much Anymore	Sophisticated Lady
Embraceable You	Stella by Starlight
Fly Me to the Moon	Stardust
A Foggy Day	Stormy Weather
Have You Met Miss Jones	Summertime
I Can't Get Started	Sunny
I Could Write a Book	Sweet Georgia Brown
If I Had You	Take Five
I Get a Kick Out of You	Take the "A" Train
I Got Rhythm	Tea for Two
I'll Be Seeing You	Teach Me Tonight
I Love You	There Will Never Be Another You
It Had to Be You	They Can't Take that Away From Me
It's All Right with Me	The Way You Look Tonight
Just One of Those Things	What Is this Thing Called Love
Lady, Be Good	When I Fall in Love

BEBOP AND JAZZ STANDARDS

The tunes listed below have been played by jazz musicians for years. Some are based on the chord changes of other standards (e.g., *I Got Rhythm*), while some are original compositions by jazz masters. Their complicated harmonies often mean that they are harder to play than most standards or pop tunes. All of these—plus many more—will be instantly familiar to any seasoned jazz player.

Anthropology
Bag's Groove
Blue and Green
Bluesette
Cantaloupe Island
Chelsea Bridge
Cherokee
Cottontail
Countdown
Cute
Daahoud
Donna Lee
Doodlin'
Doxy
Forest Flower
Four
Giant Steps
Good Bait
Goodbye Pork Pie Hat
Groovin' High
Hot House
Impressions
In Walked Bud
Joyspring
Ko-Ko
Lester Leaps In
Li'l Darlin'
Naima
Now's the Time
The Old Country
Ornithology
Our Delight
Raincheck
Red Clay
Rockin' in Rhythm
'Round Midnight
Seven Steps to Heaven
Shiny Stockings
Since I Fell for You
So What
Take Five
Walkin'
Yardbird Suite

The list below includes tunes you'll be more likely to play in a contemporary-music setting. If you are in a wedding band or a cover band, these songs are probably in your repertoire, even if you don't play them all the time. It's good to know these tunes for gigs during which a distraught bride or a drunk waves a $50 bill and begs to hear that one tune that means so much. If you play it, you'll save the day and maybe pocket a few extra bucks. Again, there are many more standards in similar styles than are presented here; these just provide a point of departure.

Back in the USSR
Born to Be Wild
Brick House
Brown Eyed Girl
Can't Buy Me Love
Can't Help Falling in Love with You
Come Together
Dancin' in the Streets
Down on the Corner
Eight Days a Week
Every Breath You Take
Get Here
Gimme Some Lovin'
Good Lovin'
Great Balls of Fire
Have I Told You Lately that I Love You
Hey Joe
Hey Jude
Honky Tonk Woman
House of the Rising Sun
I Can See Clearly Now
I Got You (I Feel Good)
I Heard it Through the Grapevine
In the Midnight Hour
I Saw Her Standing There
I Shot the Sheriff
Isn't She Lovely

Killing Me Softly
Louie, Louie
Michelle
Mister Magic
Moondance
Mustang Sally
People Get Ready
Play That Funky Music
Pretty Woman
Purple Haze
Respect
Runaway
Sittin' on the Dock of the Bay
Superstition
Tears in Heaven
Tell Me Something Good
Tempted
Twist and Shout
Unchained Melody
Under the Boardwalk
What's Going On
When a Man Loves a Woman
Wonderful Tonight
You've Lost That Lovin' Feeling
Yesterday
You Are the Sunshine of My Life
You've Got a Friend

You might be called upon to play the songs below at a jazz gig, a wedding or a pickup session. While the bossa nova style has been beaten to death by bands and has saturated the background at supermarkets, all of these songs, whether Cuban, Puerto Rican, or Brazilian in origin, sound amazing when played by musicians with an authentic Latin sound.

Agua de Beber
Begin the Beguine
Black Orpheus
Blue Bossa
Caravan
Corcovado
Desafinado
Felicidade
Flamingo
The Gentle Rain
The Girl From Ipanema
How Insensitive
Manteca
Meditation
Morning
Nica's Dream
Night in Tunisia
One Note Samba
On Green Dolphin Street
Pensativa
Poinciana
Samba de Orpheus
Sidewinder
Song for My Father
Soul Sauce (Whachi Wada)
Triste
Watch What Happens
Watermelon Man

Chapter 10

SOLOING

Every musician wants to be a better improviser, but how does one go about this? This chapter will discuss methods for coming up with new musical ideas and improving your improvisation chops. To use this chapter effectively, you must have a good grounding in music theory, including knowledge of all major and minor keys and scales, and be able to sight-read well. The more you know about music theory in general, the better you'll be able to comprehend what happens around you musically.

USING THE PENTATONIC SCALE

A pentatonic scale is any scale with only five notes. It can be a major pentatonic scale (Example 36A), which has a major 3rd, or a minor pentatonic scale (Example 36B), which has a minor 3rd.

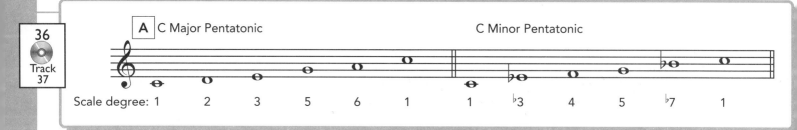

Now play up and down the major pentatonic scale, skipping every other note.

These patterns can be effective in your soloing, especially if you use them in a subtle fashion. Here's an example of a solo with some brief pentatonic phrases inserted.

The pentatonic scale you use doesn't necessarily have to be based on the root of the chord you are playing. You can use other pentatonic scales, both major and minor, on a single chord change. Here are some examples of pentatonic scales that work well with different chord types:

CHORD TYPE	PENTATONIC SCALE
C Major:	C Major, G Major, A Minor
C Minor:	C Minor, E♭ Major, G Minor, B♭ Major
C7:	C Major, G Minor, E♭ Major (for a bluesier sound)

Learn these pentatonic scales in all keys, both major and minor, then transpose these chord/pentatonic scale pairings. Writing them down will help you to memorize them.

Here's a solo that uses several kinds of pentatonic scales. Play through it to see and hear how the different pentatonic scales (marked with brackets) slip in and out of the phrase.

By this point you've hopefully recognized the merits of the pentatonic scale. You've probably also figured out that not all improvisation is based on the pentatonic scale. Did you hear how the pentatonic phrases weaved in and out of the solo above? Maybe you wondered where the other notes in the lines came from. Turn the page to find out.

The *harmonic minor* scale is a minor scale (i.e. with a ♭3) with a ♭6 and ♮7.

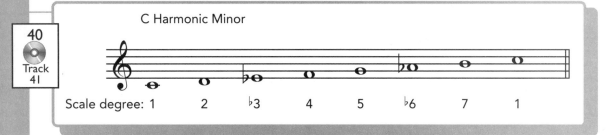

40
Track 41

C Harmonic Minor

Scale degree: 1   2   ♭3   4   5   ♭6   7   1

This scale works well in minor keys and in II–V7 progressions. In a minor-key situation, the ♮7 is the "color" tone. It is also the 3rd of the V7 chord. This note can add spice to your lines, either as a passing tone to the root (Example 41A), or as part of a line built on the V7 chord (Example 41B).

41
Track 42

In a II–V progression, or in a II–V7–I progression in minor, you can effectively use a harmonic minor scale based on the tonic note.

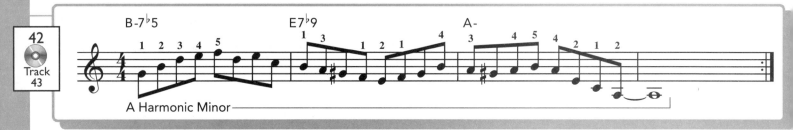

42
Track 43

Play through the exercise below, which uses the C Harmonic Minor scale in 3rds. Go up and down the keyboard with it, transposing it into all keys. Pay attention to the intervals, and experiment with them in solos of your own. A great solo is not a series of scales, but an instantly crafted melody. Use these scales as springboards, though not necessarily as models, for your own creativity.

43
Track 44

APPROACH TONES

Approach tones are the diatonic notes that adjoin (either above or below) the notes of a specific chord, most often the tonic. In the key of E♭ Major, for example, the main chord tones are E♭, G and B♭. The scale tones that precede these notes are, respectively, D, F and A♭. You may find these useful in approaching the main notes of a chord during a solo.

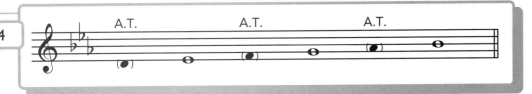

You can also use approach notes from above, in this case F, C and A♭.

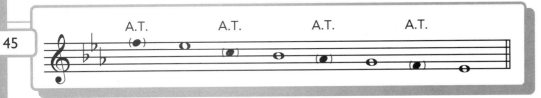

Approach tones can be effective with virtually any chord. Be sure you know which minor scale a chord is based on, as the 6th and 7th degrees can vary. The chart below illustrates approach tones for a number of scales. Practice these in all keys so you can recall them instantly. You'll find that the ability to instantly recognize and play these approach notes will stimulate your creativity.

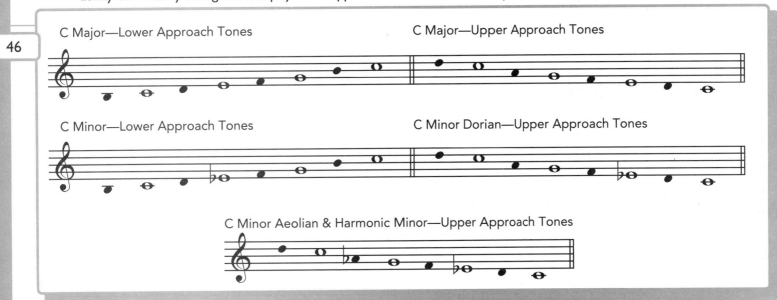

CHROMATIC APPROACH (LEADING) TONES

In using approach tones, you're not necessarily restricted to diatonic notes. Chromatic approach tones, also known as *leading tones*, can provide extra color in your solos. Play the example below in all keys, noting the placement of leading tones (marked "L.T.").

You can alter a phrase by repeating it with a subtle rhythmic variation. This technique has been a major factor in many great solos. Here's a phrase played slightly differently the second time.

Play through this example, using rhythmic variations of your own.

An easy way to practice this concept is to apply it to a blues progression. In the example below, the first phrase is repeated with some slight melodic and rhythmic variations in the second bar. Play through it and create some rhythmic variations of your own, combining them with melodic variations.

Try applying similar techniques to music you already know using one of these methods:

1. Play through the melody, giving every note a different rhythmic value from what is noted on the page. You can make each note shorter or longer, and/or your phrasing can spill over the bar into a different chord. This may give you new ideas and open up your ears to different rhythmic possibilities.

2. Play through the melody, placing an additional note between every melody note. This obviously works best on a song that isn't already full of many short notes. You can use chromatic approach notes, scale approach notes, or any other notes anywhere on the keyboard. At first, keep your note choices relatively close to the melody. After a few times through the song, try leaping up or down more than a 5th, to and from the melody note. You'll start to hear new things by using large melodic leaps.

RHYTHMIC DISPLACEMENT

Rhythmic displacement occurs when you repeat a particular phrase on a different beginning beat from that of the original. The first phrase in the example below begins on beat 1; its repetition, however, begins on beat 3.

Track 49 / 51

You can use a form of rhythmic displacement in your solos to create tension. The listener will expect the phrase to be repeated in the same place with roughly the same notes, but you can modify it as you see fit. You can repeat a phrase any number of beats away from its original starting point, e.g., 1 beat, 1½ beats, 2 beats, 2½ beats, etc.

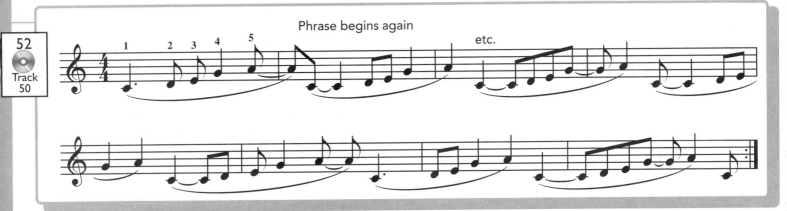

Track 50 / 52

AUGMENTATION AND DIMINUTION

There are two main ways of changing the duration of each pitch in a series. Diminution condenses the rhythmic structure, proportionally reducing the duration of each note. Augmentation does the opposite, proportionally increasing the duration of each note. In each case, the pitches of the melody remain the same. The melody below is followed by versions employing diminution (Example 53B) and augmentation (Example 53C).

Track 51 / 53

These techniques can be used to rework melodies you know and like, and to make them sound different from the way you've thought of them or heard them before. While the results may not always be to your liking or musical taste, the mastery and creative application of these techniques can open up a great many creative ideas.

Chapter 11

If you don't sing, new challenges await you. Even if you do sing, working with vocalists requires a different mindset from working with other musicians. Vocalists have to produce sound without the aid of an external instrument like a keyboard or guitar. Vocalists have no visual reference points like keys or strings to see if they are sounding the correct note. All means of musical production must entirely come from inside their bodies, and they must be fully attentive to every sensation. Because of this, vocalists can have a more difficult time than instrumentalists in adjusting to certain musical elements. Keyboardists have everything in front of them, while vocalists have to imagine and feel everything they do even before they make a sound.

WORKING WITH A NEW VOCALIST

If you are playing with a vocalist for the first time, there are a few things to know, whether you're at a gig, a rehearsal, or just an informal run-through:

1. **The vocalist must concentrate on the melody.** You have control of the harmony; the vocalist has control of the melody (assuming everything goes according to plan). Provide real support with your playing, and remain sensitive to whether your part belongs in the foreground or the background—or somewhere in between—at any given point.

2. **The vocalist will probably garner more attention than you.** This is not something to get angry about; this is just a part of the tradition of the vocalist/accompanist relationship. The vocalist has the ability to communicate not only musical sounds, but words (and meanings) as well—to literally tell the audience what the song is about. Make no mistake: your role is neither nonessential nor insignificant—just different from that of the singer.

3. **It can be nerve-wracking for a vocalist to work with someone new.** Vocalists can get very attached to particular accompanists. Some keyboard players are born accompanists and can follow singers in any circumstance. Vocalists love accompanists who can do this and will often be fond of the exact way so-and-so did it. Your tact and understanding will help in this situation. The more comfortable and professional you are, the more comfortable and professional the vocalist will be.

4. **Beginning vocalists may need help with notes.** If you are reading music in which the melody is fully notated (i.e., not a lead sheet), look for spots in the music where a melodic leap of more than a 5th occurs. The larger the interval, in general, the harder it is to sing. Put the second note of the leap at the top of your voicing; this will help keep beginning vocalists in tune. Do it subtly, as a banged-out melody note will sound more like a cue than an accompaniment.

5. **Kindness is good.** Especially if you are working with a beginning vocalist, an easygoing, helpful attitude will go far in increasing a singer's comfort level and confidence. A sincere compliment or a nice smile can have a positive effect on even the tensest, most stressed vocalist. The nicer and more helpful you are, the better the vocalist will perform. A gracious and professional singer will be sincerely appreciative of a skilled and sensitive accompanist and will generally give credit where credit is due.

6. **Less is more.** The plain fact is that a sparser accompaniment allows a vocalist or instrumentalist to be more creative with his or her part (especially in jazz). If your accompaniment is too busy, the soloist will have little space in which to work. However, a clear and concise laying down of the chords will provide a harmonic blanket through which the soloist can project. An overactive comping pattern will not be appropriate for most situations. Naturally, every situation is different, but vocalists tend to want the support of a strong harmonic underpinning.

7. **The better your transposition skills, the more effective an accompanist you'll be.** Good transposition skills are invaluable when it comes to accompanying singers. Different singers will sing the same song in different keys, and even the same singer may sing the same song in different keys on different occasions, depending on the circumstances. In pickup (unrehearsed) gigs, charts are a great thing to have, as a vocalist shouldn't expect every band member to know every song in every key. Singers should bring their own charts. If they don't have them, you can offer to write them yourself—for a fee, if you wish.

FIGURING OUT THE RIGHT KEY

Some vocalists, particularly beginners, have no idea which key is best for them in singing a particular song. They might start singing in one key but get to the middle of the song and realize that it is too high or too low. Here are some helpful hints to aid both of you in finding the proper key:

1. **Know the song yourself.** If you don't know the song or don't even have an idea of how it's supposed to sound, it will of course be harder to find the appropriate key. If you don't know a song, admit it. It's better to admit ignorance and feel a little foolish than to make a mess of things and look very foolish If you are familiar with a song's melody, you will be able to find the proper key more easily.

2. **Find the high and low points in the melody.** Using the chart of different vocal ranges on page 62, find out where your singer's best range falls. Check to see if the highest note in the song is too high, or the lowest note too low. It's usually easier to approach a high note by step than to jump to it, so if there is a phrase with a leap of a 5th or more to a note in the highest end of a singer's range, transpose downward to make it easier to approach. Also be aware that if the lowest notes are too low, they may not project well.

3. **Make sure the song is in a key you and the band feel comfortable playing in.** Many jokes have been made about the singer who calls songs in F# and B, awkward keys for most musicians. What a vocalist may not be aware of is that there is probably a key just above or below that awkward key that it is both easier for the band and suitable for the singer. For a situation involving transposition and/or musicians who might be unfamiliar with a tune, a simple half-step transposition may make the song easier to play. If possible, when you are transposing up or down a half step, choose the key (higher or lower) that is better suited to the vocalist's range.

The chart below illustrates some range guidelines for various vocal types. Keep in mind that these are approximations; while indicated limits are typical, they will vary from singer to singer.

GENERAL IDEAS FOR VOCALS

There is nothing that will educate you better than experience. You can read pages of information about what it's like being on a gig or in an unfamiliar musical situation, but you will never know what it feels like until you actually do it. Hopefully, you have already had some experience playing in such a situation. Some people actually sound better this way—it gives them a kind of rush that helps them to focus. In fact, many musicians have played their best when they weren't quite sure what was going on. Some have thought of themselves as surrendering to the cosmos or being part of a musical divine intervention. However you feel about it, the experience is what counts.

That said, how do you learn about playing with a vocalist? How do you put yourself into the singer's shoes to understand what it's *really* like?

SING IT YOURSELF

You don't have show off your vocal skills (or lack thereof) in public, but you can gain a lot of knowledge about the human voice and how it works by accompanying yourself at the keyboard while you sing a melody. Not only will your sense of pitch improve, but you will hear where your vocal range falls, allowing you to relate yourself to other vocalists of your range and type. Some keyboard players sing better when they accompany themselves, as they can control the harmony and give themselves certain notes to cue them into the right pitches. Try singing something at the keyboard and then away from the keyboard—you will likely hear and feel a difference. A keyboardist can focus on his or her instrument to block out the audience, but a vocalist does not have this option. Some, however, will use a microphone stand to comfort them and block out anything they feel is invasive, while others will use the time-honored stare focused just above the audience's heads.

Singing will give you ideas about how to comp better for vocalists. They need a gentler form of comping, one that lets them hear the harmony clearly and that doesn't get in their way. Playing with a vocalist for the first time is like having a conversation with a stranger. An ideal listener makes an ideal accompanist, just as an ideal and curious listener makes a great conversationalist. If you think of a vocalist as someone with interesting things to say, then you can set a mood that allows his or her statements to be persuasive and convincing.

Accompanying is part listening, part reacting, part feeling and part rationalizing. You listen to what is going on around you musically, you react to it in your playing, you feel the emotional and musical weight of what to play and how to play it and you rationalize what you're doing and how it affects the whole of the song you're playing. Sounds too deep? It isn't, really. Most musicians do it by instinct—which can be largely the product of experience.

Chapter 12

Sooner or later, you'll find yourself in a musical situation that is new and unfamiliar. You may have been in one already. Whether it's a jam session, sitting in on a friend's gig, or doing a gig without knowing anyone in the band (and perhaps not even the music), there are ways to relax and play well without being nervous. Many musicians say that a new musical situation makes them play better, as they focus on getting their parts right and listening to what the band is doing. There's no doubt that a little nervousness can give you an adrenaline rush and give your playing more energy and life, as well as a certain focus and an eagerness to "do the right thing."

Let's look at some different situations you might find yourself in.

ANATOMY OF A JAM SESSION

The jam session is an old tradition—nearly as old as music itself. Musicians have always gotten together to play through songs or compositions or to try out new material. A modern version of a jam session might be a group of several musicians getting together to play through songs they already know, just for fun. Sometimes musicians bring in written music or teach the other players songs; at other times, the music may be unfamiliar to all of the players. A great jam session should leave you feeling inspired and happy that you improved your musicality and playing.

What should you expect if you're called to a jam session? You should first find out the basics: who is playing, where it is, what equipment they have and what kind of music they are planning to play. If you don't know any of the musicians playing, there's no immediate need to feel nervous. Playing with new people can open your ears to new musical possibilities, as every person has his or her own unique ideas. Make sure to find out whether the venue is a club, a rehearsal studio, or someone's house, as this will suggest what equipment is available and what you will need to bring. In terms of the music itself, you probably don't want to play in styles that are completely unfamiliar to you, so make sure you'll be playing in a style or styles that you find relatively comfortable.

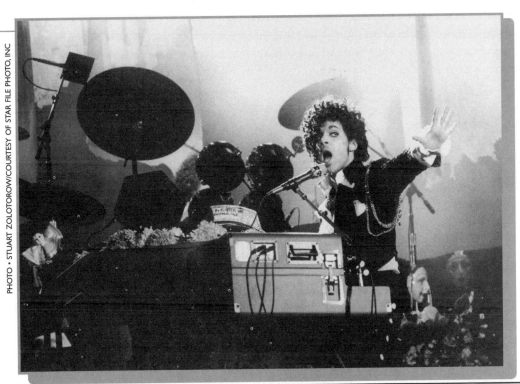

PHOTO • STUART ZOLOTOROW/COURTESY OF STAR FILE PHOTO, INC

*Though he is best known as a singer, guitar player and composer, **Prince** is a master keyboardist. The scope and level of his accomplishments have made him one of the most influential musicians of his generation.*

How you "act" at a jam session has nothing to do with making intense faces as you play a rip-roaring solo. It's about proper behavior when you are jamming with others, especially if you don't know them. Here are some jam-session tips that will mark you as a professional:

1. **Be courteous.** Many jams are ruined by the one guy who thinks he's the greatest thing since sliced bread. Such people act as though they know everything. Nobody likes them much. If you are kind and polite while being confident, not only will people play better with you, but you will play better as well—and others will like you as a person.

2. **Don't force your opinions on others.** If someone calls a tune you don't like, there's no need to yell out, "That tune is lousy!" If a selection truly offends you in some way, you can claim musical ignorance or just say you've played it too much lately and are really sick of it. The latter option is the more respectable choice, as it makes you look more seasoned and knowledgeable without being obnoxious. By the way, you should never comment on another person's playing—unless it's a form of mild praise.

3. **If you're going to play it, make sure you know it.** Usually, someone will throw to the group the question, "What do you want to play?" You can always call out a tune yourself; however, make sure you know the tune. There are few things worse than looking like an idiot by not knowing a tune you called yourself (or claimed you knew). It's no embarrassment to say you don't know a song—not everyone can know everything. Some tunes are so easy that you can pick them up quickly. Judge for yourself how to handle a song you don't really know. If you do decide to wander into unfamiliar territory and a chord change eludes you, there are a number of things that will help you. If you know how to play the bass and/or guitar, look at the bassist's fingers to determine the root of the chord, or the placement of the guitarist's fingers.

4. **Wait your turn.** Many jams at clubs allow you to play only one or two songs yourself, as there will often be many people wanting to play. Find out from the leader when you will be able to play by asking how many other keyboard players are ahead of you.

5. **Don't play for too long.** The world seems to be full of saxophonists and guitar players who play ridiculously long solos. Why join them? The best improvisers can say more in 16 bars than most people can say in 16 choruses. Keep your solos relatively short, especially if there are many people waiting to solo on the tune. A strong musical idea far outweighs a constant flurry of notes. Make your statement and get out. Always leave people wanting more.

All of the above points can be applied to any situation in which you're playing unrehearsed with other musicians. However, there are even more things to think about when you're playing with a thrown-together band for a last-minute gig. It can seem nerve-wracking, but it can actually be fun to play with new people and make it look as though you've been playing together for years. Here are some tips on how to survive and thrive in the experience:

1. **Know what tunes you can play.** Make a list of all of the songs you know, along with the keys you are comfortable playing them in. It's also a good idea to tote along to a gig any fake books you have, as a tune you don't know might get called, and a fake book will help you greatly in sight-reading. Don't forget to bring a music stand to support the book in a way that makes it easy to read.

2. **Call easy tunes that everyone knows.** It's generally a good idea to play a song that everyone knows and feels comfortable playing. Even if one chord eludes someone's memory, they can figure it out after hearing it or by looking at the bassist's hands. Easy songs are the best to play, as the musicians will be able to focus more on the music instead of searching for chords and melodies.

3. **Know your sounds!** Be aware of where the different types of sounds (pianos, organs, strings, synth sounds, etc.) are in your keyboard's banks. The quicker you can find a sound for a new section, the easier the gig will be and the better you will play.

4. **Pay attention to the other musicians.** This has already been mentioned, but if you are paying attention to what the other musicians are doing, you will be able to react appropriately to almost anything. Awareness counts for a great deal, both musically and physically. Most communication between musicians on a gig is done through visual signals, such as cueing endings and mouthing the names of different sections. If you are the leader, everyone will look to you for guidance and expect you to cue these things as well as to count off songs. Keep your eyes and ears open at all times.

PHOTO • GIN SATOH/COURTESY OF STAR FILE PHOTO, INC

George Duke has played and recorded with everyone from Miles Davis to Frank Zappa. His signature synth solos are legendary among keyboard players.

Chapter 13

One of the great things about being in a band is that you have the opportunity to write your own music and hear it played by the group. Whether you write by yourself or with a partner, the possibilities for musical expression are bounded only by your own limitations and those of your band. You'll also feel a stronger connection to the group if you can create music for all of you to play.

WHERE TO BEGIN

The first step towards successful songwriting is to find a way to make yourself do it. Schedule a time during your day that is devoted exclusively to writing. John Lennon and Paul McCartney would meet for about three hours to create songs, and they never came away from their sessions empty-handed. Here are some things to think about regarding songwriting:

1. **Just write!** Don't edit yourself as you go. Don't evaluate your work as you're creating it. There's generally no need to come up with a fully finished song in one sitting. You can always use some time at the end of your session to work on details, form, arrangement, etc.

2. **Write down your ideas, no matter how bad you think they are at the time.** An idea might seem stupid one day and brilliant the next. Creating an entire song is great practice, even if you think the result isn't very good.

3. **Record it.** With the technology so cheap and available, it's easier than ever to record yourself as you work on a song. You have no excuse not to do so. Keep a recording device on at all times while writing; even a cheap cassette recorder will work. Eventually, you'll forget it's there, and any reservations you might had about recording yourself will be gone— and no idea will ever be lost.

4. **Realize that everyone creates in different ways.** If you're writing a song with lyrics, you might work better if you write your lyric ideas first, and then set them to music. On the other hand, you might have an idea for a melody, and then come up with chords and lyrics. There's no right or wrong way to do it, and you certainly don't have to write the same way every time.

5. **Seek out the opinions of others.** Once you've got a song together, play it in its raw state for someone whose critical ear you trust (i.e., not your mom). If the song is for a band, play it for one or more of the group members. Note that letting other musicians come up with ideas for your songs is often really rewarding. Other musicians, particularly those who don't play the same instrument as you, may have a different musical perspective which may be of value. Of course, don't let someone else mangle your song or strip it of its essence.

Once you've set aside time for your songwriting, the next step is to get ideas—to get inspired. A great way to get your mind going is to just noodle around on the keyboard. Record what you're playing, of course, and don't think too much about what you're doing. Inspiration can strike at any minute. When you get what seems to be a good idea, work with it until you have several bars sketched out. Write things down if you have time, as this will save you from having to notate the music later. If one aspect of a song comes to you first (e.g., melodies, lyrics or chords), notate or record it. It's better to go with one type of idea than to wait for the song to flow out as a whole. You can fill in the rest later.

Here are some methods for developing musical ideas:

1. **Keep in mind that less is more.** You've probably heard it a thousand times, but simple ideas often do work best. As you write, don't feel as though you have to conform to anyone else's ideas of how a song should be. It's best to not let it get too complicated right away— you can always add more complexity later if you need or want to. Some songs work marvelously with only three chords, so don't be afraid to keep things simple.

2. **Create a strong chord progression.** A strong harmonic progression can make a mediocre melody sound great. It's all right at first to copy other songwriters' progressions, but try to use these only for study unless you can *really* change the song to make it yours. Charlie Parker and Dizzy Gillespie, for example, created great music in the 1940s by taking the chord progressions of standard tunes and adding their own melodies.

3. **Create a strong melody.** You'll want to create a melody that sticks in your head long after the song is over. Think of all of those catchy pop songs; note that they tend to have strong melodies, however annoying some may be. While you don't to specifically emulate songs like these, try to incorporate a strong sense of melody in your own songs. There is no recipe for a surefire melody. The only thing you can do is to listen to songs you like and figure out how and why the melodies work in them.

PHOTO • CHUCK PULIN/COURTESY OF STAR FILE PHOTO, INC

Jan Hammer's groundbreaking keyboard work with Jeff Beck and others helped create a new place for synth solos in modern music. He is also well known as a producer and composer for television and film.

4. Really develop the melody.

The best songs have a melodic statement that is worked through in a variety of ways:

It may be repeated with one note different . . .

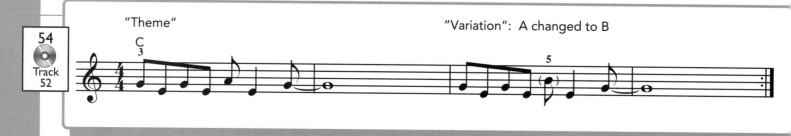

. . . or be followed with a phrase that is different (but derived from the original) in some way . . .

. . . or be followed by a reordering of its parts.

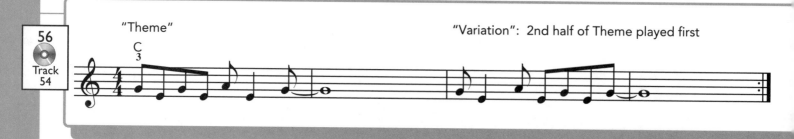

The possibilities for development are endless. Closely study your favorite songs to analyze how the melodies twist, turn and grow.

USING HARMONIC MODELS

If you're just beginning to write your own music, there's nothing wrong with drawing inspiration from and emulating musicians and songwriters you admire. If you can't come up with a melody or chord progression that sounds good to you, listen to what other artists are doing. Use their sound as a blueprint for your own creativity. Take the chords, or even the general feel of the tune, and write your own music around it. It may not be your greatest creation, but it will give you a place to start.

Take care to avoid musical clichés. In the late 1950s and early 1960s, for example, many tunes featured the same progression, the now-familiar I–VI–IV–V. When this was first played in a rock setting, it sounded new and fresh. But after everyone and his brother started using it, it began to sound dull and repetitive.

Here's a simple blues progression. Play the chords and come up with your own melodic ideas. After a few choruses, use the chords in parentheses to add some color.

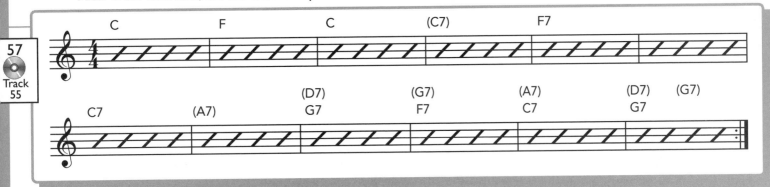

Many modern songs contain only a few chords, sometimes using the same chords with different melodies for different sections. Here are a few examples of simple chord progressions you can use. Create your own melodies to go over the chords, and don't worry if they sound like another song. This is only an exercise, so don't edit yourself. Try playing the progressions in different keys. This should automatically give you some new ideas, as musicians tend to play differently in each key.

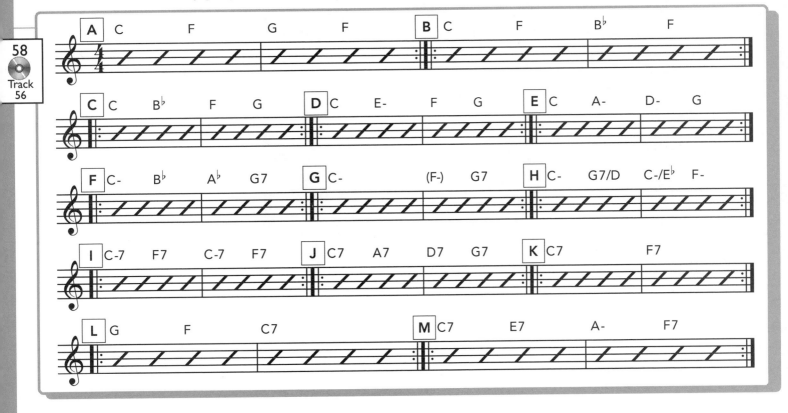

The best way to learn about bass lines is, naturally enough, to listen to bass players. Because of the physical differences between the bass and the keyboard, both instruments will gravitate toward certain phrases. Like guitarists, bass players will hear and play different things than you, and vice versa. Listen to your favorite songs and pick out what the bassist is doing. Make sure that it's a real bass as opposed to a synth bass; otherwise, you're listening to a keyboard player, which defeats the purpose.

Many tunes are built around the bass line. The bass line can be the signature element of a song, in fact, making it danceable and funky or reflective and mellow. If you can't come up with any song ideas using your synth sounds, switch to a bass patch and play around with a repetitive, low-end figure. Often, the bass line will suggest a harmonic pattern. You can take a two-bar bass line and put a four-bar harmonic pattern over it, like this:

59
Track 57

Experiment with bass lines by using chord progressions that you like, either from songs you know or your own progressions. Don't get too busy, though, as a busy bass line can overpower the rest of a song.

PHOTO • ROBERT E. TEESE/COURTESY OF STAR FILE PHOTO, INC

Herbie Hancock has proved his versatility in endeavors from playing in Miles Davis's legendary quintet to his own acoustic jazz and electric funk recordings. He was one of the first keyboard players to bring the synthesizer and other electronic keyboards into jazz.

You've probably heard of Rodgers and Hart, Lennon and McCartney, Goffin and King, Laurel and Hardy. With the exception of the last pair, they were all famous songwriting teams.

Writing with another person is a tricky thing. Both individuals bring different aspects of musicianship to the table. You might say that the whole of the duo is greater than the sum of its parts. Your partner will have ideas that you won't and vice versa. For this to work effectively, you both need to be open to each other's ideas. Assuming that you respect each other, this shouldn't be too difficult.

Here are some tips to help you and your partner work as a productive, cohesive unit:

1. **No idea is bad.** An idea may not be right for a particular song, but that doesn't mean it's bad. You should never rule out anything. The right idea will come if you give it time. If a melody or chord progression doesn't sound right in one tune, save it for another. Composers and songwriters have been doing this for centuries.

2. **Don't attack your partner's ideas.** A negative reaction to an artist's creative efforts can leave him or her bruised. If a musical or lyrical idea doesn't work for you, tell your partner tactfully. At the same time, don't be too kind if something bothers you. If your song is turning out to sound nothing like you had planned, be firm in stating your original intentions. It is your music, after all.

3. **Free associate.** Nothing is stupid. Well, *some* things are stupid, of course, but in the act of creating, you can't let anything block your imagination. Blurt out anything—you have the tape recorder running, remember—no matter how silly it sounds. There are literally thousands of successful songs whose lyrics are completely ridiculous when taken out of context, but which work perfectly within the song. Sometimes you need to drop your inhibitions in order to delve deeper into the well of creativity. The perfect lyric or chord can magically appear at any moment.

4. **When in doubt, keep it simple.** The great jazz bassist Charles Mingus once said that anyone can make the simple complicated, but it takes a genius to make the complicated simple. Often, the first chord you find is the right one. Get your music written down first, and worry about the arrangement later. You can always go back and change things, but sometimes it's best to stay out of the way and let the creativity flow.

5. **Listen to your partner when he or she has an idea.** As you're working on a song, try to provide ideas that both complement and contrast with what your partner has written. For example, an eight-bar bridge that takes a different turn lyrically or musically will add new depth to a song. One of the best things about writing with someone else is the wealth of different musical ideas you'll have to work with when you put your heads together.

6. **Write with someone who plays a different instrument.** Working with someone who isn't a keyboard player will give you a different point of view. Since guitars and keyboards are played differently, a guitarist will hear things differently from you and thus provide new insight into the music. Likewise, if you're writing with a singer, he or she will probably come up with something that wouldn't have occurred to you working on the keyboard.

7. **Contrast is good.** If your partner's melody is very rhythmic and busy, write a harmony or rhythm part that is relatively simple. Likewise, if the melody is simple, a shifting harmony or funky rhythm might complement it well. Variety makes music more interesting.

Chapter 14

ARRANGING

The art of arranging involves the creation of—surprise!—a musical arrangement for you and/or your band to follow. Arranging can be a one-person job or a group effort in which the band as a whole plays through a song and each person contributes his or her own ideas. This does not necessarily mean adding new music to what already exists; rather, it involves deciding what goes where and how this instrument plays that passage. Arranging is done after the tune has been written in its entirety. A good arrangement can make a passable song sound amazing, while a bad arrangement can ruin a wonderful song.

THE ELEMENTS OF AN ARRANGEMENT

When you arrange a song, you must approach the task from the following angles:

1. **Form.** Form in its most general sense is the whole structure of a song (verse–chorus–bridge, etc.). In arranging a song, you have the ability to enhance the music by manipulating the form according to your will. You might, for instance, decide to have the bridge come after the first verse and before the chorus, but then eliminate it after the third verse. Changes like these can create a more concise form that will keep the energy of the song afloat.

2. **Instrumentation.** While arranging for instruments usually involves just writing out parts, there is still a great deal of instrumental arranging in a contemporary band situation. It never hurts to know how jazz and classical composers arrange and/or orchestrate. A good arranger knows the ranges of all the instruments he or she is writing for, as well as how to balance them with one another. Arrangers determine which instruments are best in different roles and sections throughout a song. For example, an overdriven guitar might sound great on the chorus of a song, but if it's featured throughout the whole song, it can sound redundant, leaving no "space" in the sound. An arranger knows the instruments (and vocals) well enough to use the right sound at the right time.

3. **Dynamics.** Volumes can range from very quiet to blisteringly loud. Generally, not all songs need this wide a span of dynamic levels, but some variations should occur. A song played *pianissimo* throughout can seem boring, just as a loud thrashing tune with no letup in the volume level can become just as tiresome after a while. Contrast is the key. The intensity with which you play a song matters as well. You could be at a medium volume, while playing with an intensity that gives the music a high energy level. Think of it as being a crazy guy on the street muttering to himself. He isn't especially loud, but the intensity of his voice suggests that something is bubbling under the surface (which you hope will stay there). The intensity of this sort of mutter can be more frightening than if the man were screaming. When music has this kind of intensity in certain sections, it can add power without adding volume. This should be worked into your arrangement.

4. **Contour.** The contour of a song is its overall shape. Lower pitches and softer sections such as first verses will be lower on a contour map, while louder and more intense sections will be higher. Here's an example of such a map, with the song sections listed below.

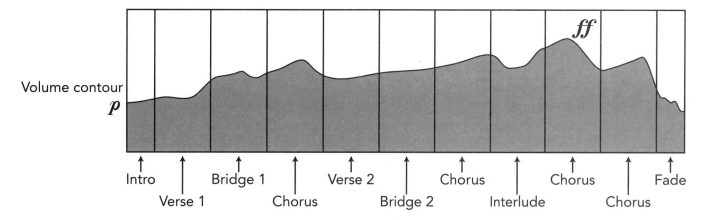

A great song arrangement has some sort of contour to emphasize the different sections. Again, not every song has to go from *pianissimo* to triple *forte,* but some changes in dynamics, range, etc. that relate to the song will make it more effective and interesting for the listener. Don't try to make a naturally loud section soft, or a soft section loud, but use a dynamic contour to build the song in a manner suggested by its melody and overall feel.

5. **Texture.** Textures are the different types of "feels" that instruments create. A picked guitar has a staccato, choppy sound, while a synthesizer pad is smoother. Part of the art of arranging is the balancing of textures, so that there aren't too many similar sounds playing at once (unless, of course, that's what is called for). A picked guitar part can be balanced by a smooth electric piano sound, while a busy and frantic drum groove can be balanced by a simpler, more legato bass part. Even though different textures should complement one another, it's not unheard of to have sections in which every instrument is playing fast and choppily; generally, though, a balance of smoother parts with choppier parts is what you want to shoot for.

6. **Timbre.** Timbre is the tone color produced by an instrument. A successful arrangement blends different timbres to create a pleasing overall tone color that works for the song. Synth timbres are often described with terms like "smooth," "shimmery," "crunchy" and "atmospheric." When you see one of these in a synth patch's name, you can imagine what it sounds like. A careful mixing of timbres in an arrangement allows for a better overall sound feel, even if one timbre, such as a distorted guitar, is the predominant sound.

Let's look at an eight-bar phrase and some different ways of arranging it. We'll assume that you have in your band a keyboard (with many different sounds available), a guitar player, a bass player and a drummer. Here's the chord progression we'll use as a basis:

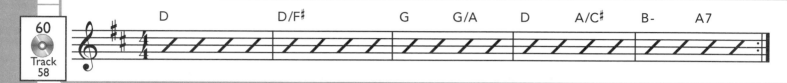

Now, let's add the band. The bass and bass drum parts should pretty much line up with each other, meaning that they should emphasize most of the strong beats together. This first example has the guitar playing a busier, staccato part, with the keyboard providing a pad-like role. Note how the guitar and keyboard parts balance each other.

This version brings the keyboard to the foreground, with the guitar sustaining the harmony.

Arrange this chord progression in a variety of settings: straight-ahead rock, R&B or even country. Write it out for keyboard, guitar, bass and drums. Go a step further and add another keyboard part. Try varying the roles between the guitar and keyboard. Let one instrument become the dominant sound with the other in a pad-like role, interlock the two parts, etc.

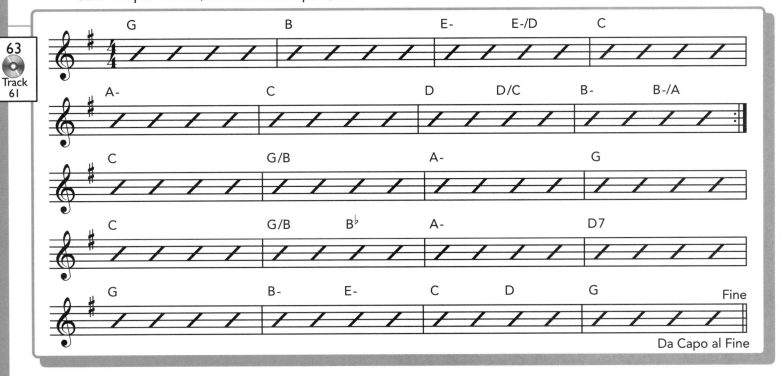

USING OTHER INSTRUMENTS

If you have a chance to write for horns, do it! Horn players can create different textures and sounds that even the best sampler can't emulate. If you really want to do a serious horn arrangement, consult an arranging or orchestration book for the finer points of writing for the instrument. In the meantime, here are some ranges of different horns and how they transpose. (A transposing instrument is one that is notated in one key, but sounds in another. For example, when an E♭ alto saxophone plays a C, it sounds an E♭.

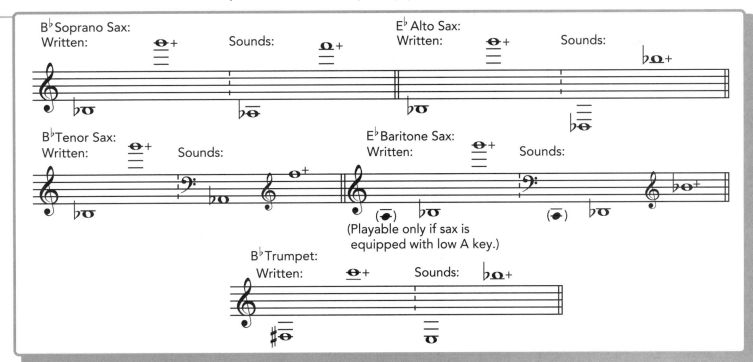

When writing for horns, stay away from voicings in 4ths and 5ths, as they can sound unpleasantly hollow. Also, minor 9ths are hard for horns to keep in tune and can sound too dissonant. The tritone makes a lovely interval within a voicing, but as the top two notes, it can sound harsh. When in doubt, keep the arrangement simple, as an over-arranged part of any sort can be disastrous to an otherwise great piece of music.

Chapter 15

Have you ever met someone with perfect pitch? Someone who could name every note you played? Weren't you secretly annoyed by that person? Well, you too can be this annoying—or at least be more annoying than you are!

A true sense of perfect pitch is innate (rather than learned) in those who have it. Maybe it seems cool to you, this ability to immediately hear and name every note, but many people with perfect pitch can tell you how harsh it can be to listen to something out of tune, or how difficult they may find it to transpose a piece of music at sight (a common issue for people with this ability).

Even if you weren't born with perfect pitch, there are still a few things you can do to get your ears functioning at a higher level.

YOUR AURAL WORKOUT

By far the best things you have going for you as a musician are your ears—meaning that you can hear music created by others and react to it in your own musical way. When you can tell which pitch a note is, you can react to it more quickly and more effectively. Use this ear-training exercise to improve your pitch recognition abilities.

If you have a recording device, set it up to record yourself playing at a piano or keyboard. If you have a keyboard, set it to a piano sound. Do the following:

1. Play a C major triad in both hands. Let it sustain for two to three seconds.
2. Let the chord go and play a random note on the keyboard, sustaining it for two to three seconds.
3. Repeat steps 1 and 2, keeping the note the same.
4. Repeat steps 1 to 3, recording as many different notes as you wish.
5. Listen to the recording, not looking at the keyboard.
6. Guess which notes are being played after each C chord. After the second time each note is played, check it against the piano. How did you do?

The C Major chord before the note gives you a tonal center to which you can relate the pitch. If the note is an F♯, the sound of the tritone between F♯ and C will become more recognizable to you the more you listen to the tape.

After you feel good with one note, move on to two, then three, then four after the chord, and on up. You will start to hear chords and melodies in relation to one another, and your instant transposition abilities will improve as well. A few minutes at this exercise each day will do wonders for your ears.

There are also ear-training computer programs available, and these can help you as much as the exercise above. With a computer program, first set it to play intervals. Two notes will play, and you will have to guess the distance between them. Then, work on individual pitches, using intervals. For instance, the computer could play C and F, and you would then have to determine not only the interval, but also the notes themselves. When you feel confident with this, set the system up so you can guess two notes at a time, then three, then four or more.

USING YOUR IMPROVED EARS

So, now you're better at identifying pitches. What can you do with these improved skills? For one thing, you're now better equipped to hear and understand melodies. If you are playing from a chord sheet, listening to the melody will give you a clue as to how to comp. Notes that stand out can be voiced and accented better when they recur. You can also correct the intonation of vocalists and non-fixed-pitch instruments—but always do so kindly!

With practice, you should be able to hear and remember entire melodies and chords more easily. A great way to check your ears is to transcribe a song's melody and chords from a recording. Transcribing is the art of listening to a piece of music and writing it down. It's better exercise to do this away from the piano, going back to the instrument to check your work only afterward. This can be difficult at first, but it gets easier with practice. You'll eventually be able to learn and transcribe tunes away from the piano—even in an elevator, if you're so inclined.

THE ART OF TRANSCRIPTION

It may seem difficult to transcribe tunes or solos from a recording, but you don't necessarily have to start with the most difficult song you've ever heard. Select an easy piece that you've always wanted to know how to play.

Here are some tips in making a transcription:

1. **Tune your keyboard to the pitch of the recording.** Not all recordings are at A=440, which is the most common tuning standard. By way of brief explanation, an A above middle C in this tuning will cause vibrations in the air—440 per second, to be exact. The number of vibrations per second is defined in Hertz (Hz), so that A=440 Hz. Figure out the tuning standard of the instruments in the song and adjust your keyboard accordingly.

2. **The bass line tells all.** If you can figure out the bass line, you will have a much easier time figuring out the harmonies. Bass players play the root of the chord at least once, as it defines the tonality. Other notes in a line will give you an idea of the chord quality (major, minor, etc.). Note, however, that just because a bass line contains a ♭6, for instance, it doesn't mean that this is the root of the chord or that it even belongs to the chord above.

3. **The melody may also contain important musical information.** The melody will normally contain at least some of the notes of the harmony. Some people prefer to learn the melody first, then the chords. As you write down the melody, be sure of the pitches and rhythms. If you're not sure of a rhythm, take down the pitches only—you can always adjust the rhythm later.

4. **Write down the easy parts first.** If you're having trouble with a particular section, leave it blank and go back to it later. The more you work on your ears, the more acute they will become. The extra few listenings you will get from going on in the tune will help you to transcribe the tricky parts later.

5. **Figure out the chords.** You'll get better at identifying chords as you transcribe. Even if you're not sure of the identity of a chord, write down what you think it may be. Again, you can always go back to it later.

LEARNING SONGS IN SECTIONS

In transcribing, you might find it easier to work on learning songs one section at a time, especially if the whole song is complicated. Breaking down a large piece of music into smaller sections renders the transcribing task much easier.

To do this successfully, you must first be able to figure out the overall form of the song. Before you sit down to figure out pitches and rhythms, listen to the song and pick out where sections begin, end and repeat.

There are a number of different song forms in common use. Some may be best described as having a verse-chorus-bridge scheme, while many songs are based on one of the standard "letter" (e.g., A–A–B–A) forms. Aural cues like hearing the title in the lyrics (which often occurs in the chorus) can be a help in figuring out exactly where you are within a song.

A few common formal schemes for songs are listed below. Most familiar songs you might want to transcribe will likely conform to one of these (or a slight variation).

A–A–B–A	A–B–A–B	A–B–A–C	A–A–B–A–C	A–B–A–C–A

Verse (V)–Chorus(C)   V–C–Bridge(B)   V–Pre-chorus (PC)–C

Intro–V–PC–C   V–PC–C–B   V–C–V–C–B   V–PC–C–V–C–B–C

FORMS AND FUNCTION

Once you've figured out the formal scheme of a song, write it down at the top of your music paper. This will help you as a kind of map and checklist to keep track of your progress on various sections. As you transcribe, you don't necessarily need to get everything down in order from beginning to end. For example, you can figure out the chorus first, and then go back to the intro or verse. Label the beginnings of all the sections on your paper, and write down the number of bars in each section.

If you aren't sure where a section begins or ends, listen for particular clues in the tune. A change of harmony plus the emergence of a new melody generally signals the beginning of a new section. If you still aren't sure, mark out a series of eight-bar segments. Most songs are structured in even-numbered sections of bars and phrases. If you aren't sure what to call a particular section, give it a letter name for the time being and figure it out later as you become more familiar with the song.

If you can figure out the key of a song, you're already on the right track. Each type of key or mode—for example, major or one of the forms of minor—has a unique pattern of chords than can be built on the successive notes of the scale. Often, a song will remain in a single key throughout, making use of chords derived wholly from that key. Sometimes, composers and performers will mix and match chords from different keys based on the same *tonic* (home note), e.g. C Major and C Natural Minor, in a single song. From there, the sky's the limit when it comes to a song's chord vocabulary. It's all a matter of the tastes and imagination of the composer.

Here's a simple chart that illustrates the chords that can be built from three of the most commonly used types of scales: major, natural minor (♭3, ♭6 and ♭7) and harmonic minor (♭3, ♭6). Play through these examples slowly and transpose them to all keys, listening attentively for the differences in quality from one chord to the next and mentally fixing the tonic (I) chord as the center of gravity for each.

C MAJOR

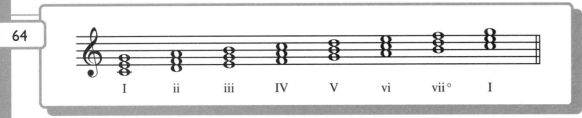

C NATURAL MINOR

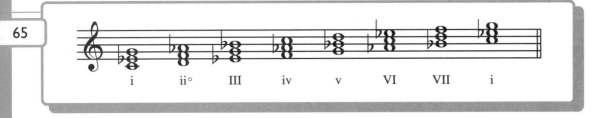

C HARMONIC MINOR

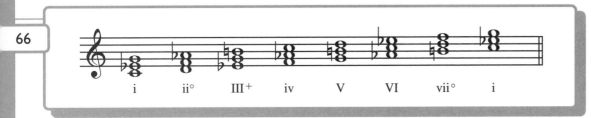

Chapter 16

PUTTING YOUR BEST FOOT FOWARD

The role of the keyboard player is different in each musical situation. He or she can be the primary sound (as in electronica and other synth-based music), play a supporting role to a guitar player (or two) or be on equal musical footing with the guitar.

WHERE THE KEYBOARD FITS INTO DIFFERENT STYLES OF MUSIC

In jazz and more standards-based music, the piano is often used instead of the guitar, or sometimes with the guitar. Jazz and other improvisational styles require that a player be particularly attentive to the other musicians. Pop, rock and R&B styles tend to rely more on "part playing"—that is, each musician has a specific part or line to play, and little variation or improvisation is involved. A syncopated comping rhythm that forms the backbone of an arrangement, for example, could be called a part.

WHAT OTHERS LOOK FOR IN A KEYBOARDIST

1. **Someone who pays attention.** A drummer whose lower jaw begins to drop halfway through a song will most probably not be concentrating on the task at hand. Not only does the music suffer when this sort of thing happens, but the audience can see the drummer's lack of effort (as well as the drool heading down to the snare drum). The best keyboard players are aware of what is happening at all times. The worst type of non-listening keyboard player often thinks that he or she is in sync with the band, but really isn't.

2. **Someone who knows the music.** It's always best to know and play your music well, but even if you're not entirely sure of all the chords to a song, play with conviction. You can always look to the guitar player to see or ask for chords.

3. **A sensitive accompanist.** When it comes to playing behind singers and instrumentalists, less is definitely more. A busy accompaniment can make it hard for the soloist to make his or her musical statement—complicated rhythms get in the way. An ideal accompanist lays down the harmonic rhythm and provides energy to fuel the soloist's ideas without overpowering them.

4. **Someone who is kind.** This does not refer to the sort of "kind" that allows people to walk all over you, but to the pleasant frame of mind that allows people to be relaxed around you. People play better when they are comfortable with the person with whom they are playing. If you show up to a gig or rehearsal with a massive ego or problem attitude, chances are that nobody will like you—or at least they shouldn't. Always maintain confidence without conceit.

5. **Someone who pays attention to volume.** A loud keyboard part is not necessarily a good keyboard part. If you consistently play louder than the rest of the band, they will soon tire of your lack of attention to dynamics. Make sure that you are at a volume equal with that of the rest of the band. Hint: Don't point your amp directly at anyone, except perhaps yourself. An amp pointed at the bass player's head will make him or her think that you are playing too loud.

6. **Someone who knows his or her gear.** If you haven't memorized where specific sounds reside in your keyboard, write down the names and locations of each patch and tape the list to your rig. If you don't want to get tape on your equipment, keep the list in your case and pull it out when you are setting up.

    As a side note: After each patch name and number, also notate where middle C is in the patch. Some sounds, such as bass sounds, are transposed down an octave or two from this C. It pays to know where your middle C is when you're quickly flipping through patches.

7. **Someone who shows up on time and ready for the gig.** It's a given that promptness is a necessity in the music world—or in any business, for that matter. Someone who is late once to a gig or rehearsal can be excused, but a pattern of lateness will lead to a bad reputation. If it is a matter of not having enough hours in the day to do everything, you might want to rethink your schedule somewhat and eliminate any parts of your day that cause eventual delays. You should also make sure that you have enough time to get to your gig or rehearsal from wherever you are beforehand. It's better to be up-front with anyone if you really can't make a rehearsal time when you say you can.

    Likewise, showing up looking right is a necessity. Even if your band doesn't have a visual image in terms of clothing, the better you look, the better you will be treated. This doesn't require you to wear an expensive suit to every gig, but do dress accordingly. A gig at a smoky bar will require different attire from a fancy gig at a country club.

GENERAL POINTS

If you are showing up to a musical situation for the first time and don't know anyone in the group, it's a good thing to listen more than speak. You will gain more knowledge about the rest of the band by watching how they talk, act and play than by gabbing about what a great gig you had last week. While you don't necessarily need to clam up entirely, the other musicians will appreciate you more if you don't try to take over the conversation or the vibe of the music.

Try to make sure that all of your equipment is in working order. Even though gear breaks down on occasion, an essentially solid rig will save you embarrassment. If something malfunctions unexpectedly, apologize and remedy the situation as quickly as possible without overreacting. If you seem as though you're about to have a conniption because of a bad cable, people will assume that you'd have an even worse reaction if a more serious problem arose.

1. **Use a metronome.** This doesn't necessarily refer to one of those old windup things that swings back and forth; nowadays, you have the option of a portable battery-powered model. If you can find one that also includes subdivisions and can be programmed for different time signatures, so much the better. You can use the metronome to beat out quarter or eighth notes. If you really want to gauge your sense of time, set the metronome to mark beats 2 and 4. This will give you the backbeat present in much contemporary music and will enable you to feel the subdivisions of the beat more easily. Your general sense of time and rhythm will improve.

2. **Slow down the tempo.** If you can't get a particular song or passage under your fingers, slow it down. If you can't play it slowly, you probably can't play it quickly. Pay attention to difficult parts that you can make your way through but could certainly play better. Isolate tricky parts and play them at half speed. Increase the tempo as you become more comfortable. When you feel good about the section as whole, play it again and add the bars immediately before and after. This will get your fingers used to the movements near the difficult parts and make the transitions between the sections smoother.

3. **Don't practice what you can already play.** Doing this isn't practicing—it's playing. It's often a good idea to go through something you already play well in order to warm up, but playing it for more than a few minutes won't accomplish much. Work on things that are not yet comfortable to you. This will make your practice time more productive.

4. **Make your practice space a calm and focused area.** Sometimes space constraints won't allow for this, but you can probably still at least arrange things around your practice area to help keep you focused. Place objects that inspire you—such as photographs or artwork—around your practice area.

5. **Work on different styles.** Variety is the spice of life, as the tired adage says, but it's true. Investigate other styles of music; they can add to your practicing and playing repertoires. If you're a rock player, learn some jazz and R&B tunes; if you're a jazz player, work on some rock and Latin songs. There's always plenty of classical music on which to draw as well—a little Bach never hurt anyone. Even if you don't use all of these different styles in your playing, familiarizing yourself with them can greatly enrich your overall musicality. Many professional musicians like music one normally wouldn't associate with their particular styles. This doesn't make their primary music weaker; it makes their ideas stronger.

6. **Sing along as you play.** Who cares if you can't sing in tune? You're practicing! Sing along with your solos as you improvise. You'll find that your keyboard phrasing will change when you sing as you play. Certain phrases are easier to sing, while others are easier to play. When your singing controls the phrasing, you come up with different rhythmic ideas, and your phrasing will also sound more natural.

7. **Avoid overuse of the sustain pedal.** The sustain pedal can act as a sort of security blanket. It can make improperly played passages sound smoother, but it can also blur the notes and harmony beyond recognition. Practice everything—especially scales and other exercises—without using the sustain pedal. This will make any technical faults in your playing stand out so that you can focus on the tricky sections. Add the sustain pedal only when you are confident with a passage and have all the notes under your fingers.

1. **Always have extra cables on hand.** Your keyboard case will probably have space for cables, so pack at least two extra ones just in case one suddenly dies or the guitar player forgets one of his own. In addition to ¼" audio cables, it is wise to bring an extra power cord for your keyboard (or any other gear that has a detachable power cord). It's easy to lose cables, so always pack backups. The nice thing about most keyboard power cables is that they are of the same size and wattage as those for other electronic equipment. When worst comes to worst, you can always use a power cable from a computer or fax machine to power your keyboard, as long as it's of the same shape. Make *very* sure that it is of the same wattage as your original cord (keyboards have their wattage listed near the power cord area), as the wrong power level can literally blow up your keyboard.

2. **Insure your gear.** Your local musician's union and other musician service groups provide equipment insurance, generally for a reasonable price. You should look for a policy that covers your gear no matter where it may be stolen or damaged. Also, you should try to insure each piece of gear for a specified amount, rather than for its estimated value. You might not always be able to replace stolen equipment easily or for the price for which it is normally covered, especially if it is no longer manufactured. Make your insured amount higher than what you think you would have to pay for it again. This can cost more in terms of premiums, but it is worth it should the worst happen. Talk to an insurance company to get an idea of how much it would cost to insure your gear.

3. **Copyright your music.** One easy (though not always legally foolproof) way to copyright your music is by placing on any written copies of your songs the word "Copyright" and the copyright symbol followed by the year in which you wrote the piece, the word "by" and your name (or the name of your publishing company, if applicable). For example:

   Copyright © 2001 by Joe Blow

   The most legally sound way to copyright your music is to submit a copyright form (which requires a fee) and either a printed or recorded version of the song to the United States Copyright Office. The ownership you will be granted is needed if you become involved in a copyright infringement case in which you believe that someone has stolen your music (or someone else feels believes that you have stolen theirs). Your music is technically yours once you "put it down" in some form (e.g., on paper or as a recording) and add the copyright symbol, but an *official* copyright gives you true legal ownership.

4. **Join a performing rights organization.** In the USA, the main performing rights organizations are ASCAP, BMI and SESAC. These entities collect royalty monies from radio and television stations and other types of businesses that utilize music, monitor broadcasts and other musical activities and distribute money to songwriters based on how many times their songs are played. Normally, you do not join all three organizations but instead select one or another. Each operates differently, so check into each one to see which is best for you. There are generally fees to gain and maintain membership, but this investment is minimal compared to the royalties one of these organizations can collect for you.

Chapter 17

UNDERSTANDING THE
MUSIC BUSINESS

The problem with the music business is that it is a business. Not all musicians are inclined toward business-related and creative matters in equal measure. Unfortunately, so many musicians have been ripped off by unscrupulous businesspeople that it is now necessary for musicians to have a good idea of how the music business works as a whole. There are so many aspects to the music business that it is difficult to cover them all, but here are some basic concepts to get you started.

GIGS AND CONTRACTS

If you are booking a gig for yourself, it is often a good idea to use a contract in dealing with your client. Your contract should outline exactly what you will need from the venue and what the venue will expect from you. Each point should be spelled out as clearly and succinctly as possible so that there won't be any questions or problems later. Make sure you get the contract to the client at least 2½ weeks before the event, and ask that it be signed and returned immediately.

A contract signed by both parties binds you and the other person(s) to fulfill all its terms and conditions. If you do not meet all the terms and conditions, the other party has the right to not pay you in full or to take you to court. However, you have the same right and can refuse to play if basic agreements are not met when you arrive at the venue. Most musicians will allow a certain leeway on some issues, such as only having three monitors onstage instead of four. Small issues can be overlooked, and they don't necessarily justify a refusal to play. However, a signed contract allows you to seek a remedy if important criteria are not met.

Not every gig will require the use of a contract. Many small clubs and restaurants don't work with contracts, since they change the entertainment frequently, and there is rarely enough money involved to warrant the time it takes to prepare contracts. Of course, be sure that the club or venue has a good reputation and has not cancelled gigs or refused to pay a band after a gig—unless there was a legitimate reason for doing so.

THE PRO KEYBOARDIST'S HANDBOOK

Here is a sample contract for a private party or wedding gig. You can use this as a template to create your own contract, adding or subtracting points as necessary.

(Your name, address, phone number, fax number and e-mail address here)

Dear John Doe,

This contract will confirm our engagement to provide music for your wedding reception to be held on June 17 in the year 2006 beginning at 7:00 p.m. We will play the equivalent of 3 sets of 50 minutes each between the hours of 7:00 p.m. and 10:00 p.m. with two short breaks of 10 minutes each, during which we will provide recorded music. Our attire will be suits and our repertoire will consist of see attached list. The band consists of Steven Jones, keyboards; Bill Smith, guitar; John Brown, bass; Thomas Miller, percussion.

As agreed, I will provide the following equipment: all musical equipment, PA system, recorded music during breaks.

You will provide the following equipment: sheltered playing area, electrical power.

Food and drink of the same quality provided to your guests will also be provided for the band (note here whether the band is to be fed free of charge, are subject to a cash bar, etc.). It is to be made clear to the caterer and/or staff at the venue that the band members are to be treated as your guests. (These items are pertinent mainly if you are playing a gig at which is food is to be served. Note that if your band consists of more than eight people, it may be difficult to get the client to agree to a "free food" arrangement.)

Our fee for this engagement will be $800.00, which includes all transportation costs. To activate this agreement I must receive a nonrefundable deposit of $80.00 by June 3, 2006. The balance is to be paid to me immediately following the engagement. If overtime is required, and if other obligations do not prevent us from continuing our performance, the rate is $150.00 per half hour, or any fragment thereof.

In case of injury or illness, at my sole discretion I reserve the right to replace any member of my group to ensure the quality of performance you have requested. Please make sure that we are advised of any special song requests well in advance. If you have more than one special request, additional rehearsal costs will apply. Also, please make sure to provide us with adequate directions to the engagement at least two (2) weeks in advance.

Please sign and immediately return both copies of this agreement to me along with the deposit. I will countersign and immediately send one copy to you for your files. If the deposit is in the form of a check, please make it payable to Steven Jones.

If you should have any further questions, feel free to contact me via the information above.

Sincerely,
Steven Jones

Accepted by (X) _____ dated February 1, 2006

Address_____

Telephone _____

At the dawn of the 21st century, the music business is in a strange state of flux. Technology is changing everything so fast that information quickly goes out of date. Some people think that record companies as they currently exist may become a thing of the past in a few years. Many people are creating their own music from start to finish and marketing it over the Internet, achieving sales without the help (or hindrance) of record companies. It is impossible to predict what the future holds for the music business.

Currently, the major record companies are the biggest manufacturers and distributors of recorded music. They essentially function as banks. When you sign a contract with a record label, you will receive a loan that pays for recording, promotion, distribution and tour expenses. The label will also give you an advance—money to cover your living expenses and studio time. The good thing about an advance is that if your recording doesn't earn enough to cover this amount, you don't have to pay it back. On the downside, the label will probably drop you, and other companies may be afraid to pick you up.

You really don't earn anything from a recording until it sells enough copies to cover the company's investment in you, including your advance. If the recording recoups this initial investment—which does not always happen—the earnings from that point are divided between you, the record company and others (the producer, for example). Hopefully, your contract will assign you a healthy percentage of these profits—your royalties.

THE RECORD DEAL

When you sign a contract with a record label, it is an exclusive deal, which means that you will not be able to record for any other labels or projects without the record company's permission. Labels will often try to sign you to a multi-record deal. A lot of new artists are offered a five- or six-record deal, but this is not necessarily a good thing, as there is no guarantee that your label will actually put out every album—or even your first one. The streets of major cities are overrun with musicians and bands that signed a deal with a label only to be dropped from the label even after making a recording (and some don't get that far). Record companies can entangle you in red tape, keeping you entirely out of the loop as to what they plan on doing with you. Labels want to sign you to multi-record deals because if you do well, they will have a contract with you that keeps you tied to the deal—which, in turn, makes them more money. Sound evil? It sure can be.

The main reason to play music is to express yourself artistically and emotionally—not to make all the money you can, though that is a nice benefit. If you want a large, guaranteed income, don't look to a record contract to fulfill that dream. So, how *do* you actually make money with recorded music? Aside from earning royalties or performing live in support of a recording, there are other ways to generate income:

1. **Publishing.** If you want to write music only for yourself or your band to perform, you will probably just need a publishing company of your own. You will need to set this up through both a performing rights organization (ASCAP, BMI or SESAC) and the government. Starting up a publishing company usually means incorporating yourself in some way. A knowledgeable and trustworthy lawyer may be well worth the expense to ensure that all legal bases are covered.

   If your goal is to write songs for other people, you might want to try to get a publishing deal with a major publishing company. The goal of this plan is to place your songs on as many albums as possible and thus make as much money as possible. If your record label's publishing company insists on owning part of your songs—something you should aggressively resist—make sure that they don't cross-collateralize your publishing and recording accounts. Cross-collateralization means that a record company can deduct monies from your publishing proceeds if your record sales are not as high as expected.

2. **Merchandising.** Most of us have t-shirts or posters of bands or artists we like, and a lot of the money spent on these goes to the artist(s). Record companies might try to take control of your merchandising, but if you control it yourself, the profit margin can be very high. A t-shirt with your band's logo might cost just five dollars to make, but you can sell it for 10 or 20 dollars. The only costs to you should be those involved in manufacturing and selling your merchandise.

PROMOTION AND DISTRIBUTION

If you have a recording of your music, you want to get it out for everyone to hear, right? This may involve the services of a distribution company. The major labels and their subsidiaries all have their own distribution companies or rely on a larger, outside distribution company to put their products on the street. Small and independent labels use independent distributors to get their stuff out there. Some will use one distributor for one part of the country or the world and another for a different area, according to a distributor's strengths in certain markets. Distributors take a portion of your profits for this service. While it should guarantee that your recording will be in major stores nationwide, it doesn't guarantee that it will be advertised. This is where promotion comes in. A record company or distributor will market a type of music to an area that would be likely to favor a certain CD; for instance, country music is promoted more heavily in the South, while R&B is promoted more heavily in urban areas. While this may seem like stereotyping, the figures don't lie—certain types of recordings do sell better in certain areas than others.

A promoter will hype your record for a fee and try to spark interest in it. The best promotions are those in connection with performances by you and your band. A successful promotion makes the public aware of your music through advertising in print, radio, TV and other media. It costs more to hire a promoter, but it can be worth it if you achieve greater sales.

LAWYERS

Unfortunately, lawyers are a necessity in the music business, but a good one on your side can get you a good record deal. Labels look at you first as a potential profit-making enterprise, not as a great band or musician that everyone should hear. An entertainment lawyer who works for you in securing the best deal possible is a valuable asset. Be sure you at least get a lawyer you trust to review a record contract before you sign it. Recording (and often, other music-related) contracts are full of legalese and mumbo jumbo. Your lawyer should be able to explain each item in a contract in clear English.

THE SHAPE OF THINGS TO COME

In the end, many people take a piece of the financial pie that your music generates. It may seem unfair, but it is the system you're stuck with for the time being. The record industry has been run like this for decades, but there is a ray of hope in the rights that artists have won in the past few years. The continuing evolution of on-line commerce, the rise of file-sharing technologies and services like Napster, the regular introduction of all-new media, and musicians (like Prince, for example) who bypass major labels in producing and distributing their music all suggest that artists are posed to become a more powerful force in the business end of the recording industry than ever before.

Chapter 18

It's ideal to have someone represent you as an artist. If you have just started out as a band or as a solo artist, you will do fine booking gigs on your own, but as your career progresses you may find it necessary to obtain a manager. This person should not be in the band, but should have a close connection to the band. He or she should have good business sense, with a good idea of how the music business works. This manager could be a friend of the band, someone recommended to you by another band or someone whose opinion you trust in general. In any case, there are a number of things that any good manager should do:

1. **Book gigs—ideally, increasingly better gigs— for you**
2. **Make sure you are paid for each gig**
3. **Scout around for (and stimulate) interest from record companies**
4. **Protect *your* interests in business dealings**
5. **Take care of business in general so that you can concentrate on your music**

Here's a list of qualities and qualifications a manager should possess:

1. **A manager should be friendly but firm.** Someone too hard-headed will turn people off, while someone too soft won't command respect (and will probably get you gigs that no one else wants to do).

2. **A manager should be knowledgeable about many aspects of the music business.** The music business gets more and more confusing and difficult to navigate every day, so the more a manager knows—about contracts, bookings, record deals, etc.—the better off you'll be and the more you'll be able to focus on your music. If you or your manager are in doubt about any aspect of the business, there are many books available that go into the finer points. Be sure to get up-to-date information, as the industry changes so quickly that a five-year-old book is essentially out of date. You can always track down information on the Internet, but be sure to look at official sites—not, for instance, one created by a disgruntled crank who was kicked out of a band 20 years ago.

3. **A manager should be accessible.** "Accessible" in this case means simply that if your manager isn't traveling with you, you should still be able to reach him or her within minutes—via e-mail, telephone, fax or some other means. You'll find that communication with your manager at a moment's notice is indispensable, whether he or she is negotiating a contract for you in Los Angeles (while you're in New York), or you're stuck in a blizzard in Peoria and don't know how you're going to make it to your next gig.

4. **Above all, a manager should be trustworthy.** If a manager brags about cheating someone else in order to get you better gigs, who's to say he or she won't cheat you as well? Donald Passman, noted music lawyer and author of several books on the music industry, has pointed out that someone who keeps telling you how honest he or she is usually isn't honest at all. Ask to review your manager's business records from time to time, and make certain that you are constantly updated on any new deals. You should know *exactly* where all your money comes from. If your manager hedges or procrastinates in telling you, ask pointed questions—and reevaluate your association with him or her. Unscrupulous managers have cheated many musicians out of their hard-earned money. Managers like these will always try to explain or justify why your money has "disappeared." Become as familiar as you can with the different aspects of the music business so you can ask your manager specific questions—and will know when you're being cheated.

Your manager should have more contacts in the business than you do. Otherwise, what do you have to gain from the relationship? In terms of fees, a manager will typically ask for 10–20% of the overall gross on any money *he or she makes for you*. This latter point (in italics) is particularly important—any money you make on your own should not be taken by your manager as a fee. Many managers will want you to let them handle *all* bookings and business deals. This is fine, but only if the manager has your complete trust.

In general, a manager should not ask for money up front except in the case of small expenses related directly to you or the band. Giving a manager money up front will never ensure gigs or contracts, but an ideal manager will use his or her contacts in the music industry to get you publicity—and, hopefully, gigs and recording contracts.

A manager should not take a large percentage of the gross pay for a gig if it's under a certain amount. A typical bar or club gig will not pay much, and if a manager takes a cut of this, you will be left with a very paltry sum. It's best to agree on a set fee that the manager will receive for booking low-paying gigs. This has the added benefit of encouraging the manager to book better gigs for you, if only out of self-interest. A manager should not be paid for any gigs, contracts, etc. that were in place before he or she came into the picture. However, if a manager can obtain a better deal for you at a venue where you've already been booked or on a pre-existing contract, he or she should certainly be given some form of compensation.

PHOTO • COURTESY OF THE INSTITUTE OF JAZZ STUDIES

*Over the course of five decades, **Keith Jarrett** has moved with ease between the worlds of jazz and classical music. His exceptional talent as an improviser is evident in recordings that range from the famous* The Köln Concert *to the piano concerti of Mozart.*

Chapter 19

Keyboards, especially pianos, are particularly physical instruments. They require you to use many muscles in a proper manner and order. If you use a muscle incorrectly or don't use it when you should, you run the risk of pain and injury. The basic principle involved in playing a keyboard requires you to overcome gravity. All of your movements need to be supported by a fulcrum, which is a resting point upon which something can balance. The piano stool itself is a fulcrum, holding you up. In turn, the back supports the shoulders, which support the arms and so on. All motion needs to be supported by the back, hips, stool and, finally, feet.

Here are some typical injuries that can occur from improper technique at the keyboard.

SORE WRISTS

Wrists are meant to move up and down, not from side to side. If you repeatedly try to move your hand sideways from the wrist, you will experience pain sooner or later. The trick is to make all of your sideways motion come from the elbows and shoulders, with your back supporting all movements. Your wrists can also sustain pain and injury from hard attacks on the keys, using your wrists for most of the force. The muscles in the wrists are small and cannot take the excessive force that the larger muscles elsewhere can withstand. If you allow the radius/ulna joints (the joints just in front of your elbows) to swing from side to side, the wrists can move up and down. Let your wrists swing up and down freely and slowly, following the contours of the musical phrases. Make sure they don't flop up and down.

SORE SHOULDERS

If you have problems with your shoulders, you are at least moving your pains further back into your body—which actually puts you on the road to eliminating them altogether, if you learn to make your muscles move correctly. The problem is that larger muscles take longer to heal. However, there are some ways of alleviating shoulder pain.

TOP OF SHOULDER

Even though a nice massage feels good and relaxes aching muscles, it won't solve your problems. The root of just about any continued muscle pain is improper movement, and the only cure is to correct the motion. If the tops of your shoulders hurt, you probably aren't letting movement from the other muscles in your arms pass through them.

Try the following exercise. Place your left hand under your right forearm. The left arm should act as a fulcrum, supporting the right arm. Slowly swing the left arm in a semicircle, supporting the right arm. Don't let the right arm move itself. Make several full rotations, continuing the exercise until your shoulder is relaxed and carrying the movement of the entire arm. Repeat the exercise in the other arm. This will help to relax the lower back as well.

MIDDLE OF SHOULDER

The previous exercise will also work the middle of your shoulder, but you can also use the following exercise to stretch the middle out. Use the same windmill pattern as in the previous exercise, but apply it to your shoulder blade. Hold your arm in front of you so that your hand comes up to the middle of your head. From your elbow, start the rotation—first clockwise, then counterclockwise. With your free hand, reach behind your back to touch your shoulder blade—make sure that you are using the muscle and that it is stretching out. Do at least 10 rotations each way, then do the same thing with the other arm. Be sure to use the shoulder muscles, or you will just be causing tension in the top of the shoulder.

SORE BACK

If your back hurts from playing, it could be the result of something more serious than just poor posture and/or technique. If the pain continues despite the use of the exercises described below, consult a doctor—preferably, an arts injury specialist. These professionals watch what you do and analyze your playing from a physiological and artistic perspective. They can see if you're not performing correctly, then offer solutions to aid in recovery and prevention of further injury. If you're not acquainted with an arts injury specialist, call the local musicians' union or look in the telephone book, as these doctors are often located in areas with high concentrations of musicians.

Try the following exercises to stretch your lower back. Sit on a piano stool or bench (as if you were about to play) and slowly move your torso forward from your hips. Stretch your back until your chest is touching your knees, then slowly move back, making sure that the base of your spine is controlling all of the movement. Slowly repeat this several times. Another thing to try is to lie flat on your back on an even, comfortable surface. Slowly raise both of your legs, controlling the movement from the base of your spine. Bring the legs back down slowly; try not to tighten up the back, but let it control all of the movement. Slowly repeat this several times. This may hurt for a little while, but it will relax your spine and allow it to control the rest of your body when you are playing.

GEAR-RELATED INJURIES

Roadies were invented for good reasons. They carry your stuff and set it up and do a million other things as well. Since most of us are not fortunate enough to have a personal, full-time roadie, we have to carry our gear ourselves. Musical equipment can be heavy and bulky, and if you carry it incorrectly, you can do damage to your muscles and ligaments. Be sure to lift your gear from the feet and legs, not from the shoulders. Try not to be in a hurry when carrying gear—you're more likely to pick up something incorrectly or bash your hand against a stairwell when you rush. It can be a drag to carry your own stuff, but a little extra care can save wear and tear on your body. For instance, gloves can ease the pain associated with gripping large items, and a dolly or handcart can be of great help when you have heavy things to carry over a long distance. You can find a decent handcart at a hardware store. Buy it! You won't regret it.

Chapter 20

Ah, the prospect of touring. The cities where nobody's heard of you. Extended periods of time in a van with your band mates, who may have less than satisfactory personal hygiene. Bad food. Living out of a suitcase for weeks on end. *Really* bad food. Never knowing quite where you are. And the list goes on.

Seriously, doing out-of-town gigs is a great way to introduce more people to your band's music. There's nothing that sells a CD faster than a good band playing live. If you are able to string together a few out-of-town gigs in a row, you have a tour—a minor one, but a tour nonetheless. Here are a few things you should know about touring:

1. **Think big—even if it's small.** Unless you have a huge following in the areas you're playing, there may not be a whole lot of support for your band at the gig. Even if the promoter worked like crazy to advertise you everywhere, you're not guaranteed a packed house, because most people won't go to see a band—especially if they're paying for it—unless they know something about them in advance. What do you do if there's no one at a show? Play even harder. If you act miserable on stage, people probably won't like you. Treat a small audience like you would a large audience, even if you think that going through your act for only five people seems silly. Not only is this good for the band's morale, you might also make a good impression on the venue staff and the promoter. Consider this: The Police had an audience of fewer than twenty people at their first gig in America, and they went on to become one of the most successful bands in history.

2. **Traveling is not easy.** While some people find great solace on the road, others find monotonous travel and erratic schedules unbearable. If you are in the latter group, there are effective ways of dealing with the difficulties of life on the road. (See p. 94 for more on this topic.)

3. **There is usually little financial reward when you first start touring.** If your band is relatively unknown, your first few tours probably won't make you much money. What money does come in from the gigs gets eaten up by gas, food, lodging and other expenses. One idea is to start by doing small weekend tours for which you are out of town for two to four days and play only a few gigs. This way, you won't have to travel far, and you'll play in places that are relatively close to one another.

4. **You'll find out things about your band mates that you never knew before.** A long drive may reveal to you that your bassist snores or that your drummer doesn't consider deodorant a necessity. These little unpleasant truths will come out in various ways and at various times. The best thing to do is to stay relaxed and take everything in stride while calmly addressing the problem at hand.

5. **At first, touring is not glamorous.** It's only at the higher levels of the music world that you'll find more pleasant travel conditions and comfy tour buses. For those in the lower echelons, touring can be quite boring. One reason that so many musicians became alcoholics or drug addicts is that they looked for a way—albeit an unhealthy way—to escape the boredom of the road. Bring books, crossword puzzles or video games. The more you're prepared for the road, the easier your travels will be.

A tour manager is someone who travels with you on the road. He or she deals with performance venues in advance and coordinates all your traveling details to ensure that everything is arranged and set up correctly. Your manager can also serve as your tour manager, especially if you're a relatively new band. The advantage to this arrangement is that he or she is already familiar with the band and its inner workings, so if your manager is able to travel with you, this is probably the best choice.

On shorter or smaller-scale tours, you might not need a tour manager, especially if money is an issue, since tour managers make about the same percentage as managers (roughly 10–20%) for their work.

A tour manager should have the same qualities as your manager, particularly a keen sense for detail. He or she will have to be on top of what's happening at all times and know what to do if the club owner is lying or if your written directions say one thing and the guy at the gas station says another.

Here are some other necessary characteristics of a good tour manager:

1. **Patience.** A *lot* of patience. The tour manager usually makes the first contact with the performance venue and the person or people in charge of the venue. The venue's management may be very easy or very difficult to work with, but no matter what, the tour manager must use discretion and maintain a professional and calm demeanor.

2. **A working knowledge of psychology.** A good tour manager knows the band members' idiosyncrasies, as well as what they need to help them play better. Of course, this can only be taken so far; a small venue will probably be unwilling or unable to supply the drummer with the exotic cheese he wants. But if the tour manager knows the little things that can help to make the musicians' lives easier, he or she can be of great service.

3. **A good sense of direction and geography.** This will come in handy when the directions you got from the club say that the venue is two miles from the highway, while the map says it's more like fifty. The more the tour manager knows about the lay of the land and how long it takes to get from point A to point B, the better off you'll all be.

4. **A strong knowledge of gig contracts.** If a venue's management claims they can't provide something that was a condition of the contract they signed, the tour manager should be able to produce the contract and wave it in the boss's face until he or she agrees to fulfill his or her obligations. Your option then is to refuse to play the venue until the conditions are met. (See Chapter 17, *Understanding the Music Business*, for more on this topic.)

5. **The ability to be relaxed yet focused.** The life of a tour manager is rarely stress-free. There are countless details to remember, and a tour manager who can't handle the pressure will likely vent his or her frustration on anyone nearby. A good tour manager will be friendly but firm on important points such as departure and arrival times. It's not easy to deal with musicians, so the tour manager who can be laid back while still concentrating on the particulars will do the best job.

The following is a list of things you should consider bringing with you when you're traveling. Not all of these are essential, and you might even find some of them useless, but it will probably be helpful to refer to this list when you're packing for a trip, whether it's for a weekend or for several months.

1. **A portable tape or CD player with headphones.** This will allow you shut out the world and your band mates if you have to. (You *will* have to, and they will have to shut *you* out at times.)

2. **Earplugs.** The constant noise of motor vehicles can be disturbing, consciously or subconsciously. If you want to sleep or just focus on something else, earplugs are a good way to block out extraneous noise. Standard foam plugs are available at hardware and sporting goods stores, or you can opt for a custom-made set. These are more expensive, but they are built to fit your ears and can have a noise reduction of 10–30 dB. They are also better than the standard kind in that while lowering the overall sound level, they still allow you to hear nearly all frequencies. (Earplugs are also very good for loud gigs.)

3. **Something to read.** Reading is a good way to take your mind off the band. It's also one of the best ways to cure boredom, which is an inevitable part of being on the road. Even if you're the type that can't read in a car or van, do some reading after the gig or before you go to bed. It doesn't have to be a book about music; often, reading about another subject will help you address your music better and more clearly.

4. **A journal or diary.** Even if you're not the diary type ("Dear Diary: Today I wanted to kill the bus driver"), a notebook is a good thing to have. You can use it as a way of remembering different gigs, recording your thoughts on the music, making set lists, scribbling down lyrics or just venting about the conditions. You should feel safe in your notebook. On a cramped and busy tour, a notebook is sometimes the only place you can hide.

5. **A music notebook or blank music paper.** This will allow you to write down any musical ideas instantly. Sometimes, the very presence of music paper will give you some great ideas. Write down everything that comes to you, even if you think it stinks. You might change your mind later.

6. **Water.** It's important to keep yourself hydrated while traveling. Carry either a pitcher with a water filter or a plastic bottle you can refill at rest stops. Not getting enough water can lead to grumpiness and moodiness. Your body will thank you if you keep it supplied with plenty of water. (Your bladder might *not* thank you, but that depends mostly on whether you can pull over a lot.)

7. **Anything that keeps your mind occupied.** As noted above, books, notebooks and a personal stereo will go far in alleviating the tedium of travel. Boredom leads to fatigue, which leads to poor performance. If you can find a project to work on while you're on tour, your mind will stay sharper and clearer. Learn another instrument, take up sewing, study nuclear physics, write a book. Anything that demands some concentration is better than sitting in a car watching the scenery go by in a daze.

8. **Anything that will provide some physical activity.** Carry a jump rope, a football or a Frisbee. Chances are, your touring life will consist of a lot of sitting, and the only exercise you'll get is from carrying your gear into the venue. (If you have roadies, you can't even rely on *that* for exercise.) Any form of exercise is great. At rest stops, play a game of catch or run around the parking lot. Get your blood flowing. If your hotel has a pool or an exercise facility, use it. Swimming is a particularly good exercise for musicians, as it doesn't cause the muscular strain that running can.

Again, you might not think that you need or want these things, but they represent a minimal financial investment, while their benefits greatly outweigh the cost. The important thing about being on the road is that you have to stay sane. Any of these items can help you accomplish that.

When a group of people is in a small space for a day or more (or less), the conversation, such as it is, may slowly degrade in its content and tone. There's something about life on the road that can cause people to start speaking in a manner that would shock their spouses and kids. It may be a generalization, but a van full of musicians can become a very crude and vulgar group, however saintly they may be in other circumstances. An all-male band will likely be more coarse than a co-ed outfit, as the presence of both genders tends to keep certain types of conversation from taking place. (It has been claimed that all-female bands can be just as raunchy as all-male ones, but the author cannot vouch for this statement.)

While not all of your conversation on the road should be about dialectical materialism or the triumph of the will, it doesn't need to dissolve into toilet humor, either. You might find yourself saying things you normally wouldn't say, or at least thinking them. This is normal. But you don't necessarily need to verbalize these things or act them out.

It's also important to remember that not everyone wants to hear talking all the time. People who monopolize the conversation in a car can be very annoying. The sound of silence from everyone in the car can be a wonderful thing. Chances are, someone has heard all your jokes already, anyway.

If you find that someone in the band is causing offense at times, it doesn't hurt to take that person aside and ask him or her to refrain from saying certain things in your presence. This approach is more effective than shouting at the person in the van. Always try to resolve problems diplomatically. If something negatively affects someone in the band, that negativity will come out in the music. As the saying goes, "Do unto others as you would have them do unto you."

PHOTO • CHUCK PULIN/COURTESY OF STAR FILE PHOTO, INC.

*Keyboardist **Keith Emerson** broke new musical ground with his trio, Emerson, Lake and Palmer. His fusion of rock and classical styles influenced musicians and wowed audiences throughout the 1970s and beyond.*